CLINT EASTWOOD

2

www.pocketessentials.com

Tel.
or 023

First published in Great Britain 2002 by Pocket Essentials, 18 Coleswood Road, Harpenden, Herts, AL5 1EQ

Distributed in the USA by Trafalgar Square Publishing, PO Box 257, Howe Hill Road, North Pomfret, Vermont 05053

A CIP catalogue record for this book is available from the British Library.

ISBN 1-903047-81-1

2 4 6 8 10 9 7 5 3 1

Book typeset by Pdunk
Printed and bound by Cox & Wyman

This one is for my uncles: Gene, Jack, Alan & Noel
My original band of brothers

Acknowledgements

Thanks and a tip of the Stetson to: Jeanine Basinger, Michael Connelly, David & Alexis Downs, Paul Duncan, Kirsten Ellis, Michael Goldfarb (nice lead!), Howard Hill, Steve Kallaugher, Ion Mills, Paul Shienfeld, Richard Slotkin, Adrian Wootton, Steven, Susan, Cynthia, Julie, Mikey, Alison and Andrew.

Word Of Warning

"People will sometimes put the wildest interpretations on something you've done. Whatever they say, I say 'that's right.' It's their participation that I want. What counts is it gives them their best enjoyment."

Clint Eastwood, 1988

CONTENTS

Introduction: Man With A Known Name

"He's controlled in such an uninteresting way; it's not an actor's control, which enables one to release something – it's the kind of control that keeps one from releasing anything."

Pauline Kael

"He seems to be thinking and feeling nothing, and is therefore almost invisible to the camera."

Richard Eder

"[*High Plains Drifter*] is a Middle-American R-rated substitute for *Deep Throat*."

Judith Crist

Not for the first time in the history of film criticism, these critics got it wrong. Clint Eastwood stands unique in the history of Hollywood, and his career must now be regarded as one of the most important in the history of cinema. He is a compelling presence as a male star. Many actors would be satisfied with creating two lasting franchises (The Man With No Name and Dirty Harry), but Eastwood used that success to propel himself into a position of autonomous strength within Hollywood as a director and as head of his own, successful production company. He has continued to refine and explore the natures of his two best-known personae, exploring them, playing with them and sometimes even parodying them. After all, who would really want to spend their life repeating "make my day"?

He is thought of as the ultimate action star but he has just as often confounded his audience's expectations as met them. Bronco Billy, dreamer, plays against Philo Beddoe, redneck buffoon. Sensitive photographer Robert Kincaid plays against cold killer William Munny, just as surely as the racial inclusiveness of his films and their increasing concern with family values play against the perception of him as a violent film-maker and political reactionary. He has become the image of the American hero.

There has never been a star of such stature, at the top of the box-office rankings for the best part of three decades, who at the same time has been a constantly working director (22 films in 30 years, directing himself in all but three).

It's as if John Wayne were also John Ford or, better, Raoul Walsh, because Eastwood's directing output resembles the work of a contract director in the heyday of the studios. Eastwood's production company, Malpaso, functions like a mini-studio, providing projects for Eastwood the director, and roles for Eastwood the actor to work with directors he trusts (usually himself). Malpaso produces one product – Clint Eastwood films – and has been phenomenally successful, being responsible for something like 20% of Warner Brothers' profits in the time they worked together.

At 71, an age where most action heroes are long gone, Eastwood continues to dash, if somewhat stiffly, across our screens. The anti-hero of the No Name films, the loner of the Dirty Harry films, the outsider of so many other films, has become the idol of critics, a cultural treasure. Even ruptures in his private life have done nothing to dent that image; in that he remains unique as well. As David Thomson noted shrewdly, 'actors with "distinguished" careers – Beatty, Hoffman, Redford – dwindled or stalled, while the ostensibly "lower class" Eastwood has learned, improved, developed and become one of the most respected and loved figures in American film.'

Of course, like whores and politicians, even movie people become respectable if they hang around long enough. But the upward curve Thomson applies to Clint the actor is also true for Eastwood the director, whose very best work began in his late 50s.

If the success of Eastwood as a producer has given him freedom to explore his screen persona in ways ignored by other iconic figures, and to make offbeat films without commercial potential because they interest him, it has also meant that, like an old-time studio mogul, he has consistently avoided box-office poison by giving the audience what he thinks it wants. More often than not he has been right. It is a fact that for most of his career, Clint's most successful films at the box office have been his least challenging artistically. Clint the director sometimes took a back seat to Clint the producer, and directorial reins on such commercial efforts were often handed to members of his stock company. Yet, he also gave screenwriters Michael Cimino and Richard Tuggle their first chance to direct, and they created some of his best work. He is also willing to sit on a good script, like *Unforgiven*, until he feels he is ready to direct and, as an actor, is right for the part.

Clint the director, while aware of all the nuances of his on-screen personae and willing to explore those in film after film, has sometimes found it difficult to adapt them to other genres. Also, he has often stood back from taking that personae over the edge, hence pushing Clint the actor beyond what he thinks his limitations are. When he does push, something as fine as *White Hunter, Black Heart* is the result.

The final key is control. Hollywood is a battle for control (and failing that, a battle for money and credits). Richard Slotkin said, "that notion of artistic control is really critical to his best work." Just as his characters often battle to achieve, or return to, complete control, so too does Eastwood the film-maker. The buck stops with him. In that sense, his work is incredibly easy to judge because what is on the screen is his. Over the years, although we may have been pleased, entertained and sometimes surprised by the avenues he pursues, we have rarely been shocked or stunned by those choices. Often we've thought Eastwood the artist has stepped back from the abyss. The director in *White Hunter, Black Heart* castigates his writer: "You let 85 million popcorn eaters pull you this way and that way." Eastwood often says he chooses his projects simply because they interest him but, as a producer, he has shown a canny eye for making sure the popcorn eaters regularly get what they are looking for.

So we come full circle. This book was originally limited to Eastwood the director, but taking him in isolation from his other roles as star and producer is fruitless. The themes and characters he has developed remain remarkably consistent with those formed in the films of the two great directors under whom he apprenticed: Sergio Leone (*A Fistful Of Dollars*) and Don Siegel (*Dirty Harry*). So, too, are the films he has made with other directors, whether inside or outside the Malpaso framework. They all reflect specific elements of an acting and directing style, and a specific production philosophy. These elements define the cinema of Clint Eastwood.

The Eastwood Touch

Eastwood's films have a B-movie production ethos. Malpaso productions have kept alive the low-budget style of film-making Eastwood learned early. Don Siegel was a master of making the most out of a little, and Leone started with surprisingly small budgets but produced films that looked much more expensive. Eastwood's no-nonsense approach results in films with a wider-reaching sensibility than Siegel's and, though his slow pacing and broad landscapes are often compared to Leone's, they are accomplished through different means and for very different ends than Leone's.

His early experience at Universal-International in the 1950s was also important. Patrick McGilligan pointed out their strategy relied on building cheap unknowns into popular stars, exploiting location shooting, especially on Westerns, and making gimmick pictures like those starring Francis the

Talking Mule or Bonzo the chimp (where President-to-be Ronald Reagan got to play second banana to his fellow primate). With Malpaso using lesser-known stars and distinctive character actors, and keeping a stock company together by promotion from within, they can work cheaply. Location shooting keeps costs and schedules down.

Early in his career, Eastwood cited Hitchcock as a major influence. Since then the names that come up most frequently are Howard Hawks, Anthony Mann, William Wellman, Raoul Walsh and Frank Capra. All hard-working professionals, able to work in any genre, not afraid of action. The dark side of James Stewart, which Mann used, and the populist side of Capra, are visible influences on Eastwood.

Eastwood's strength as a film-maker is that he incorporates these values into his aesthetic. It is one of the reasons he has 'learned, improved, developed.' Just as Clint was transformed from B-actor to star, or from star to director, or from action director to Oscar winner, so his films are consistently concerned with transformation.

Transformation, Rebirth, Redemption: Eastwood's concern with the individual being transformed goes well beyond the usual growth and change you would expect from plot development. In virtually all Eastwood movies, the transformation takes the shape of a rebirth, and often it involves redemption, an act which will put right the mistakes or missed opportunities of the past. Clint's characters are rarely concerned with transformations beyond themselves. Occasionally the character will take another character under his figurative wing, but secondary characters change as a process of osmosis (Whit in *Honkytonk Man*, Schofield in *Unforgiven*), while the effort to change society is fruitless. Although this element of transformation is a big factor in Leone's films with Clint, the difference is Leone's heroes are sited within their own moral universe, virtually oblivious to the outside world. This was the starting point for the classic Eastwood hero.

American Loner: There is still no better description of the American hero than DH Lawrence's of James Fenimore Cooper's Deerslayer: 'the essential American soul is hard, isolate, stoic and a killer. It has never yet melted.' With variations on the relative hardness, Clint has played that character throughout his career. He explored it first with Leone. The Man With No Name was everything Lawrence imagined and more, because the facade of civilised respectability which also defines Cooper's character disappeared in the European context of the Spaghetti Western. Eastwood played an anti-hero, a killer whose claim to white-hat status was not based on moral superiority to the villain, but on superior skill. The timing was perfect. America was ready for anti-heroes and appreciative of their 'cool,' and no one had more cool than Clint.

10

No American director was more devoted to the personality of the loner than Don Siegel. His heroes were always at odds with their society, often with their colleagues and partners. In Siegel's hands, Eastwood's Man With No Name got a very American, urban, context. As Peter Bogdanovich said, *Dirty Harry* "firmly established (his) enduring non-Western persona. Eastwood became the world's favourite loner."

Eastwood returned repeatedly to those two characters. Without stretching a point very far, he has played The Man With No Name and Dirty Harry at least ten times each. As quintessential American loners, both heroes exist outside the system, usually holding a barely-disguised contempt for it. They spend more time, and far more energy, snarling put-downs at useless bureaucrats than pumping magnum slugs into criminals. This anti-hero, even when parodied, played for laughs or exposed as a house of cards, continues to strike a chord with the public.

The Man With No Name was used crudely in *Paint Your Wagon* and *Kelly's Heroes*, and seemed relatively lost in *Two Mules For Sister Sara*. He adapted himself to the rules of American frontier society in *Hang 'Em High*, *Joe Kidd* and *High Plains Drifter*, in all three cases almost specifically addressing issues from the Leone films. Perhaps the Union corporal who wanders into the girls' school in *The Beguiled* is a survivor of the last battle in *The Good, The Bad And The Ugly*. In *Pale Rider* he revisits Western cinema, giving *Shane* an almost postmodern fantasy spin. He acquires a family in *The Outlaw Josey Wales*, then gives them up to reclaim his old self in *Unforgiven*, thus anchoring the Leone hero once and for all in the mainstream of the American Western.

Eastwood played the prototype for Dirty Harry in *Coogan's Bluff*, transforming a cowboy into an urban detective. He played variations on the Harry theme in *The Gauntlet* (Drinking Harry), *Tightrope* (Filthy Harry), *City Heat* (Thirties Harry), *Pink Cadillac* (Skip Tracing Harry), *The Rookie* (Daddy Harry) and *In The Line Of Fire* (Dirty Old Harry). His burglar in *Absolute Power* turns Dirty Harry into Don Siegel's Charley Varrick. And he brought the character full circle, revisiting Walt Coogan as Red Garnett in *Perfect World*.

Actor As Image: If there is no equivalent in movie history for Eastwood's parallel careers as actor, director and producer, the closest comparison may be the great comedians of the silent era: Charlie Chaplin, Buster Keaton or Harold Lloyd. Later Jerry Lewis took control of his films (Richard Thompson and Tim Hunter point out the close parallel between Lewis' apprenticeship with Frank Tashlin and Eastwood's with Siegel). Mel Brooks had a brief period with some control, and the nearest contemporary example is Woody Allen. Like Eastwood, Allen works in two recurring strands, a comic (Jewish) New York and a tragic (Waspy) New York, but within those strands he remains, recognisably Allen. It has to be that way, because the special control those comics achieved was largely the result of specific screen images, carefully defined and nurtured, self-controlled and, above all, inimitable. This is exactly what Eastwood has done with his own screen presence, something no other 'serious' star had managed.

When he got his first chance to star, his understanding of what he did best as an actor gave him an opportunity to mould his part. He looked for less, cutting his own dialogue to a bare minimum. He was confident in his screen presence, and in Leone he had the perfect director to use that presence, highlight it and make it do more. Likewise, Siegel saw the potential in that style and used it as a foil for his own dynamic storytelling. Eastwood's face became one of the most expressive in cinema. It was a lesson he never forgot. He continues replacing words with action, replacing action with gesture.

Richard Burton grouped Clint with actors like Spencer Tracy, James Stewart and Robert Mitchum, saying that they all shared a quality he called "dynamic lethargy." He said, "They appear to do nothing, yet do everything. They reduce anything to an absolute minimum and it's enormously effective."

Actor As Actor, Control And Denial: Clint started out as studio beefcake, part of a talent programme whose participants called each other "meat." His striking looks got him there and got him his break on *Rawhide*, where he was rarely challenged to do more than look good and ride. Even Leone was at first taken primarily by Eastwood's angular body and feline grace.

His looks are central to his acting strategy. Notice how many chances he gets to display his naked body, to demonstrate his ability to run, to conquer other physical activity. (Except throwing. From the turtle in *The Beguiled* to boom boxes or grenades in *Heartbreak Ridge*, he throws like a girl.)

Yet has any star with such an image done so much to deny his looks? He learned in the Leone films he could project his attraction right through ratty beards and stinky cigars. Dirty Harry wore a professor's patched tweeds, softening an action hero's dynamic. In a number of films he adopts disguises; he seems to love that chance to escape his personality without losing control of it. He worried playing opposite Chief Dan George: "I thought, God, how am I going to keep my composure if he's going to tug at me like this." It's rare that Clint the actor is allowed to lose his composure.

If a star acts by 'being' then Clint is more willing than most stars to direct himself into 'being' something different. If Clint as actor/director is John Wayne merged with Raoul Walsh, then perhaps it is instructive to compare him directly to Wayne. Wayne's popular image was perhaps created by John Ford, but it was developed in his lesser films, while Ford and Howard Hawks explored its more interesting facets. Wayne, as jobbing actor, or in projects he controlled (and indeed directed), was content to massage that image. Clint's image, in contrast, was created by the two top directors he worked with, and he explored it from the start in projects he controlled. Wayne waited until *True Grit* for parody, Eastwood was parodying himself quite early. Interestingly, Don Siegel gave Wayne his elegy, in *The Shootist*.

Wayne, famously, complained in a letter that Eastwood's Westerns weren't about the West at all...that they ignored the issues of pioneers which made the West what it is. This surely is the difference between the classic and modern Western film reduced to a nutshell.

Moving Camera: The common opening of an Eastwood film involves the camera panning across a landscape, often with figures already in motion. If the landscape is urban, that shot will usually be a helicopter night shot, revealing the city as a dense landscape.

In general the movement in Eastwood's films comes from the camera far more than from the editing. He will increase the pace by putting the camera in motion, rather than cutting more quickly between shots. He uses handheld cameras frequently, not only for motion but for close-up effect, and when Steadicam was developed he was quick to seize on its mobility to his advantage. Clint's set-ups emphasise intrusion into static situations, allow for its resolution in a group dynamic and highlight the entrance and exit of the protagonists.

An anonymous questioner during Clint's *Guardian Interview* pointed out his movies never ended on a freeze-frame. I'd suggest motion continues within the shot, and by implication beyond the film. Clint said they just shot until the film runs out.

Actor's Director: The moving camera also allows longer takes and more opportunity to let actors relax within the framework of their roles in a scene. Since Eastwood is often both actor and director, this frees him to concentrate on his part within the basic shot blocked out for the moving camera, leaving its success in the hands of a (trusted) cameraman, and cutting down on additional shots needed to fill the scene. Clint regularly saves his own shots for the end, allowing the other actors to stay fresh while he directs.

Eastwood shares a characteristic common to actors who direct – a tendency to let takes go long. This strategy lets his actors feel they can showcase their craft. It allows the director a minimum of fuss, while the actors get space to play around the star's considerable presence. The success of *The Bridges Of Madison County* is based on the tension between Meryl Streep as an actress and Eastwood as a star.

The notoriously efficient and workmanlike atmosphere of his sets shows the respect Eastwood is given by his fellow actors. Clint famously rolls film on rehearsal, preferring spontaneity to perfection and as few takes as possible. It's a jazz ensemble attitude. Morgan Freeman explained, following his interview at the NFT, that he felt this grew from Clint's own experience as an actor. Clint had worked with directors who knew what they wanted, yet allowed actors space to create within that framework as long as they kept things moving. Freeman pointed out that *Unforgiven*'s relatively slow pace as a story fitted the pace of Clint's takes. More to the point, he said he'd agreed to do *Under Suspicion* with Gene Hackman simply to recreate the kind of atmosphere they'd enjoyed on *Unforgiven*.

Landscape, City On A Hill: The film settings are given resonance by Eastwood's cutting pace. In his urban movies, the city is often portrayed as a collection of dark man-made mountains, casting even darker shadows. Think how many of his urban films open with helicopter night shots, placing you above the city and safe from it, at least until you venture down into the shadows. This is a pit, shot first from above and then from within, in a landscape which allows little sun and no horizon.

Open spaces hold freedom, if not promise. If the mountains which surround the characters appear to hold them in place (making some sort of confrontation inevitable, like a city's buildings), they also allow the presence of light and offer some sort of escape, perhaps, on a long road leading off into the distance. Note how *A Perfect World* opens with both the wide open spaces and the urban nightmare.

Country exteriors usually feature a backdrop of earth colour (either plains, dust or rocks) set against vibrant blue (sky or water) which gives the effect of an abstract painting. The towns are situated like forts, isolated outposts, often in the mountains or, memorably in the case of *High Plains Drifter*, by a lake.

The man-made structures are set within that landscape to make a pointed contrast between their formal shapes and the natural abstract. They are very much American, as opposed to, say, Leone's Mexican borderlands. They are proper little societies, not chaotic clusters of anarchy as in Leone. Eastwood's towns have officials and pecking orders, and they reveal interiors darker than any modern city.

Light & Dark: It is no coincidence that Eastwood's favourite director of photography has been Bruce Surtees, known in the trade as "The Prince of Darkness," and that Jack Green walks in his dark footsteps. Although Surtees has shot films bathed in light (*Beverley Hills Cop* or *Blume In Love*), most of his work with Eastwood features a saturated palate, muted colours and often sepia tones.

In his Westerns, interiors are dark, often lighted from one source, as they might have been at the time. There is a heavy reliance on backlighting, which makes the foregrounded character stand out, while reducing the rest of the cast to shapes. Even exteriors, which Eastwood likes to shoot in autumn, take advantage of nature's natural backlight.

Backlighting is put to similar use in more modern contexts as well. This sense of substance, of the exterior rather than interior working of the character, is one of the defining motifs of *Bird*, as if Charlie Parker's mind is too much for us to be able to comprehend.

If the abstract painting of an Eastwood horizon does appear in an urban film, it will be for contrast. In Siegel's *Escape From Alcatraz*, Surtees' sunsets behind San Francisco Bay are used to contrast with Morris' stay in the pitch blackness of solitary confinement.

The dark interiors of his Western outposts are also masculine. There is no change of palette to recognise that these places have acquired the trappings of civilisation, which in Westerns usually means white women.

Women: The most noticeable thing about the women in Clint's films is how many of them aren't really there. They are memory or motivation. He inherited this from Leone, whose West included very few women (and who edited out two Clint sex scenes from three films), and Siegel, for whom women characters are generally problematic. Before the film starts, or as soon as it begins, they die (*Unforgiven, The Outlaw Josey Wales*), run off (*Tightrope, Play Misty For Me*) or divorce him (*Heartbreak Ridge*). Those encountered in the films fall into four broad categories: Waifs, Whores, Wise Old Women and Working Wannabes.

The Waifs are ethereal, sometimes offbeat girl figures who are usually overwhelmed by the presence of the loner hero. Sondra Locke, of course, is the prototype waif. Whores are also commonplace, distinguished from waifs by a cruel practicality which ensures they should not be trusted. It is interesting to watch Locke's progress from waif to whore through the Eastwood oeuvre. Wise Old Women are mother figures who are scrappy, salty and aren't at all impressed by the Eastwood hero's macho bluster (Grandma Sarah in *Josey Wales*, Ma in the Philo Beddoe films).

The most interesting group, however, are the working women, who often do men's jobs or take men's responsibility. They are, at times, presented as wannabe men and, sometimes, as asexual beings (spinsters or even, in smaller roles, lesbians). Clint's masculine sexuality will often transform these women into waifs (note in *Tightrope* how the Geneviève Bujold character avoids this because of her own straightforward sexuality, or how Patricia Clarkson in *The Dead Pool* fights, as an actress, against her character's transformation). In Siegel's films such women often harbour immense reserves of repressed sexuality, which springs forward when motivated by jealousy.

In Clint's movies, that repression eventually dissipates, as he becomes more and more sensitive to women's liberation. There was the Madonna/whore dichotomy in *Play Misty For Me*, then the whore avengers of *Unforgiven* and then the working equal of *In The Line Of Fire*. The avenging woman of *Sudden Impact* kills her rapists with impunity.

The Malpaso Stock Company: Eastwood works repeatedly with the same people, giving his films a consistency of look which is unusual nowadays. His stock company of character actors resembles John Ford's. Geoffrey Lewis and Bill McKinney are his Ward Bond and Victor McLaglen, the former adding a wide range and the latter specialising in madmen and bullies. In the early years, Albert Popwell was his Woody Strode, George Orrison his Jack Pennick.

The same applies to Malpaso crews. Bruce Surtees started as his cameraman of choice, picked up from *Joe Kidd*. Frank Stanley shot some pictures while Surtees worked elsewhere, and second unit cameraman Rexford Metz took over. Camera operator Jack Green eventually replaced Surtees as cameraman of choice. Editor Ferris Webster, best known for his work with Peckinpah, gave way to his assistant, Joel Cox. Art director Alexander Golitzen worked with Clint and Siegel at Universal, gave way to Edward Carfagno, who became the long-term production designer, before being dropped from *White Hunter, Black Heart* because Clint felt he was too old. Henry Bumstead, who had designed *High Plains Drifter*, and is scarcely younger than Carfagno, came back for *Unforgiven* and has worked ever since. After working with jazz-oriented composers like Jerry Fielding and Lalo Schifrin, Eastwood began using jazz arranger Dee Barton, before finally settling on old Army pal Lennie Niehaus, a former aide to Fielding. Assistants have worked their way up to producing jobs, especially since Clint began taking producer credit for himself.

The changeovers in personnel have not been accomplished without antagonisms. Old friend Fritz Manes found himself gone as producer, perhaps because as an ex-Marine he was more popular than Eastwood among the Marines on the set of *Heartbreak Ridge*, or perhaps because he worked too hard on Sondra Locke's project *Ratboy*. Malpaso crews work regularly, but at relatively modest scale. Manes and director James Fargo both sought fees closer to the going rate, and never worked for Eastwood again.

Even those people quoted critically, particularly in McGilligan's negative biography, always seem to mix affection and respect with their criticisms of Eastwood as studio head. Working relationships are always fraught in Hollywood, and it would be childish to expect Malpaso's to be all sweetness and light. The mere fact that the stock company remains intact, and produces quality pictures, speaks volumes. Yet a future as a Hollywood mogul, Oscar-winning director and international superstar would have seemed far-fetched indeed to the youngster who grew up primarily in Oakland, California, and the Pacific Northwest.

The Early Years: A Perfect World?

Clinton Eastwood Jr. was born 31 May 1930, at St Francis Hospital in San Francisco. At 11 pounds 6 ounces, he was the largest baby most of the maternity nurses had ever seen. The proud parents, Clinton Sr. and Margaret Ruth Runner, were childhood sweethearts who hailed from Piedmont, a suburb of Oakland, just across the Bay.

Clinton Sr. moved the family up and down the Pacific Coast, holding a succession of jobs, from bond salesman to gas station pump jockey. Family ties were close; Clinton Sr. worked for a time for his brother, and the family eventually returned to Piedmont when Clint was ten, to live in a house bought at a bargain price from an aunt. Clint's biographers argue about the nature of his upbringing, about whether or not his working-class credentials are authentic. That doesn't matter. The lessons of the Depression clearly influenced the young Clint, and the early years on the move probably contributed to his independence and restlessness in both his personal and professional lives. Similarly, his feel for the tastes of the core audience, and the relative lack of artistic pretension (and seemingly, lack of worry about the critics) may also have its roots in the very straightforward nature of his non-academic education.

He began high school in Piedmont, but transferred (perhaps as the result of trouble) to Oakland Technical, where his main interests were cars and girls. He was not a joiner, did not play organised sports, but he did act in one school play, an experience he claimed nearly put him off acting forever. Tall, well-built and strikingly handsome, Clint's hair was swept back in a pompadour and he wore white T-shirts and jeans–Hollywood would later discover this type of teenager and cast James Dean in the role. Clint appears to have been the central figure in a small group of friends, who used the friendly Eastwood house as headquarters. In a pattern that repeats, members of this group continued to play a part in his life. One, Fritz Manes, became an important part of the Malpaso stock company.

The one piece of furniture that moved with the family was his grandmother's upright piano, which Clint learned to play, aided by his mother's collection of Fats Waller music. It's interesting to think of the outdoorsy

Eastwood remaining in to practise, in private, on the piano. In 1946, he was mesmerised by a Jazz At The Philharmonic concert at Oakland's Shrine Hall, seeing the stars of the new bebop movement, especially Charlie Parker. That love of jazz would stay with him. He and his friends began taking weekend trips to the jazz clubs of Los Angeles; on one of these trips they rounded up stray horses belonging to Howard Hawks, whom Clint either saw or met.

Clint played the piano for tips at the Omar Club in downtown Oakland, which was a largely black area. Playing helped build his confidence, and also attracted the girls; he learned then about the appeal of artistic sensitivity, especially when it came from such a macho-looking youth. Clint's parents moved to Washington before his senior year but Clint stayed behind, living in a friend's house until he finished high school. Then he moved north and worked in a variety of jobs: lifeguard, in paper and steel mills, lumberjack and for Boeing Aircraft in Seattle. He considered enrolling in college to study music but the Korean War interfered and he was drafted in 1951. It was a blessing in disguise.

Clint was assigned to Fort Ord, near Monterey. Because of his life-saving experience he spent his Army service as a lifeguard and swimming instructor at the base pool. Among his fellow recruits were a number of actors: Norman Barthold, Martin Milner and David Janssen. Barthold, then the most successful of the group, apparently encouraged Clint to consider Hollywood. Also passing through Fort Ord was Lennie Niehaus, who had played and arranged in Stan Kenton's band. Clint was a bouncer at the base officers' club where Niehaus played, and also travelled to the alto player's local gigs.

When Clint was discharged he returned to Seattle and contemplated resuming his education. An Army friend, Chuck Hill, recommended Los Angeles City College. Clint had been on a blind date with a Berkeley co-ed named Maggie Johnson and, after graduation, she returned home to the Los Angeles suburbs, so that may have been a factor. In September 1953, Clint enrolled in a business administration course (James Dean followed a similar path at UCLA). He found an apartment where his rent was reduced in exchange for serving as manager and, in an echo of his father, worked nights in a gas station. In December, he and Maggie were married in Pasadena.

Bored with business studies, Clint began taking acting courses at LACC, which had a fine reputation. He began hanging around the Universal lot, which was where Chuck Hill was now working. After talking to cameraman Irving Glassberg about swimming (lifeguarding sure is lucky!), Glassberg brought him to the attention of director Arthur Lubin, who arranged a screen test. Clint was hired, with Lubin as his agent, for Universal's talent development programme.

Apparently two screen tests were shot: the second, suggested by a woman impressed with his looks, was done virtually naked and convinced Universal of his potential.

Although Clint didn't reap the rewards for a long time, the Universal programme was to prove crucial to his development, and he learned lessons that would stay with him for the rest of his career.

Universal Soldier

"They had the studio system…somewhat inadequate for training actors, but you could learn something along the way."

- Clint at his AFI awards ceremony, 1995

The early 1950s were the last gasp of the old-style studio system, and Eastwood would be among the final products of studio group schooling. It was a valuable apprenticeship.

Eastwood received some first-rate acting lessons. Among his teachers was Jack Kosslyn, who would eventually become casting director for Malpaso and take bit parts in a number of Clint's films. His fellow students included his Fort Ord buddy David Janssen, John Saxon, Grant Williams, John Gavin, Brett Halsey, Barbara Rush, Gia Scala, Mara Corday and Mamie Van Doren. Of these, only Saxon later appeared in a major role in a Clint movie and Janssen would have the biggest success, on the TV series *The Fugitive*.

The programme had produced Rock Hudson and Tony Curtis, who were among Universal's biggest stars. Visiting lecturers included Marlon Brando. Between Hudson and Brando lies the full spectrum of 1950s leading men. On the one hand, method actors were alternately introspective and exploding with simmering energy, projecting insecurity, and on the other hand were the rock-solid leading men with a similar unsureness about their whole identity (think of Hudson opposite Doris Day). Eastwood says he felt Brando "looked down on acting as something he shouldn't be doing as an American male" and Eastwood thought it was "not a terribly masculine thing to do." Clint's masculinity was a throwback to heroic figures like John Wayne and Gary Cooper, yet he never wanted to follow that tradition.

19

Besides, Universal had no John Wayne roles available. Their sub-Rock Hudson heroes stretched little further than John Wayne's sometime punching bag in John Ford's Westerns, John Agar, who starred in the first of Clint's six film appearances for Universal.

Revenge Of The Creature (1955)

Director Jack Arnold, with John Agar, Lori Nelson. Eastwood (uncredited) plays Jennings, a lab technician, who thinks a lab rat was eaten by the lab's pet cat but finds the rat very much alive and in his pocket. This was his first, and biggest, part at Universal. The rat in the pocket would make a return appearance in *Escape From Alcatraz*. Alexander Golitzen served as Art Director on most of these Universal features and would work frequently for Clint in Malpaso's early years.

Lady Godiva (1955)

Director Arthur Lubin, with Maureen O'Hara, George Nader, Victor McLaglen. Eastwood plays a Saxon. Buddy Van Horn, who would figure large in Clint's stock company, worked as a rider on this film.

Tarantula! (1955)

Director Jack Arnold, with John Agar, Mara Corday, Leo G Carroll. Eastwood (uncredited) plays a bomber pilot. This is the film playing on the television in *The Rookie*, when Lara Flynn Boyle realises the man in her house is not a police lieutenant. Mara Corday would go on to play bit parts in a number of Eastwood films.

Never Say Goodbye (1956)

Director Jerry Hopper, with Rock Hudson, Cornell Borchers, George Sanders, Ray Collins, David Janssen, Shelly Fabares. Eastwood (uncredited) plays Will, another lab assistant. Clint was outfitted with horn-rimmed glasses, to make him appear more intellectual. Rock Hudson took one look and decided his character needed glasses too. After many tests, it was decided only Clint's glasses would do, so Clint played the scene without them. One can't help but think Clint's attitudes toward 'star' behaviour were already being formed.

Away All Boats (1956)

Director Joseph Pevney, with Jeff Chandler, George Nader, Julie Adams, Lex Barker, Richard Boone, Keith Andes, Charles McGraw, John McIntire, Jock Mahoney. Eastwood (uncredited) plays a sailor.

Star In The Dust (1956)

Director Charles Haas, with John Agar, Mamie Van Doren, Richard Boone, Leif Erickson, Coleen Gray. Eastwood (uncredited) plays a ranch hand.

Universal released Eastwood from its development programme in October 1955 – he was the only one of the male stars to be let go. He also broke off his agenting agreement with Lubin and wound up going through a number of agents in the next few years. He made valuable hook-ups with his business manager, Irving Leonard, lawyer, Frank Wells, and publicity agent, Ruth Marsh, at this time. Lubin held no hard feelings and gave Eastwood work on two of his pictures for RKO.

The First Traveling Saleslady (1956)

Producer/Director Arthur Lubin (RKO), with Ginger Rogers, Barry Nelson, Carol Channing, James Arness. Eastwood plays Jack Rice.

Escapade In Japan (1957)

Producer/Director Arthur Lubin (RKO/Universal), with Teresa Wright, Cameron Mitchell, Philip Ober. Eastwood (uncredited) plays pilot One Dumbo Victor.

To make ends meet, Maggie worked as a model, and Clint did odds jobs, including digging swimming pools. Among his friends doing the same work were Bill Tompkins and George Fargo. Tompkins would double for Eastwood and act in *Rawhide* and the first Leone pictures, while Fargo would also play bits, and his son James would become a Malpaso director. Eastwood also managed to land some jobs in television. His first TV appearance was on Steve Allen's *Allen In Movieland* while still under contract at Universal. Now he picked up spots on *Reader's Digest*, *Highway Patrol*, *West Point*, *Navy Log* and the Westerns *Death Valley Days* and *Wagon Train* (the model for *Rawhide*, the series which later made him famous). Then he did a film with a Hollywood legend: 'Wild Bill' Wellman.

Lafayette Escadrille (1958)

Producer/Director William Wellman (Warner Brothers), with Tab Hunter, Etchika Choureau, Marcel Dalio, David Janssen, Paul Fix, Bill Wellman Jr., Jody McCrea. Eastwood plays George Moseley. This was Wellman's last film. He later claimed its failure drove him to early retirement. Wellman had been keen on Clint for a role, but wary of his size. In a variation of an old actor's joke, when he asked Eastwood, "How tall are you?" Clint replied, "How tall is the guy?" When Tab Hunter replaced Paul Newman as the star of the film, height consideration caused Eastwood's role to go to old buddy David Janssen, but Wellman found a smaller part for Clint. This began Clint's long friendship with Wellman and his family.

Universal hadn't seen Eastwood as a potential Western star, probably because they focused on his good looks and thought of him in terms of their beefcake leads like Hudson or Curtis. Westerns were in a boom period on television and Eastwood had done a number of them, so it probably seemed like a good idea to accept a role in another feature.

Ambush At Cimarron Pass (1958)

Director Jodie Copeland (Regal/20th Century-Fox), with Scott Brady, Margia Dean, Frank Gerstle, Dirk London. Eastwood plays Keith Williams. First-time director Copeland worked on a minuscule budget and it shows, especially the distinct lack of horses. This is reputedly Eastwood's personal nadir. He has called the film "the worst Western ever made," which is harsh, but not that harsh.

Move 'Em, Move 'Em, Move 'Em: The Rawhide Years, 1959-1966

In the wake of *Ambush At Cimarron Pass*, Arthur Lubin helped Clint again. Lubin was directing episodes of the highly-rated Western series *Maverick*, starring James Garner, and he got Eastwood a substantial role as a villain in one episode. Lubin was also responsible for the next big break of Eastwood's career, through his secretary, Sonia Chernus, who later became Clint's story editor. While visiting Sonia at CBS, where she was creating the hit TV show *Mr Ed* with Lubin, Eastwood was spotted by executive Robert Sparks. Eastwood and Sparks went to meet Charles Marques Warren, creator of the long-running hit Western series *Gunsmoke*, who was producing a new Western series called *Rawhide*. Although Clint thought he'd flubbed his audition by ad libbing the dialogue he'd been given, they were more interested in his appearance and he was hired to play Rowdy Yates, the ramrod on a cattle drive.

Clint famously referred to his *Rawhide* years by characterising Rowdy Yates as the "idiot of the plains," and certainly there was little to set *Rawhide* apart from the run-of-the-mill Westerns of the time. They were incredibly popular. Even so, besides Eastwood, James Garner and Steve McQueen were the only stars who went on to film success, while many others, like John Russell (a Clint favourite), Clint Walker, Will Hutchins and Nick Adams, never impacted the big screen.

Rawhide attracted many talented actors and directors. The latter were a mix of Hollywood veterans (Richard Whorf, George Sherman, Stuart Heisler and Clint's friend from Universal, Jack Arnold) and younger apprentices (Andrew V McLaglen, Ted Post and Buzz Kulik). Eastwood is easily bored so, rather than spend his days idling, he began to study the way the programme was made. Unimpressed with some of the directors, he pestered the producers for a chance to get behind the camera, but that was not commonplace then and he did nothing more than direct promos and trailers.

Rawhide also started him on a singing career. TV stars crooning (or crooners-turned-TV stars) were popular, and Rowdy did a few turns as a singing cowboy in the show. In 1959 Clint recorded an album called *Cowboy Favorites*. Two of the songs were written by Sheb Wooley, one of the actors on *Rawhide* but better known as the singer of the hit song 'Purple People Eater.' Clint and Wooley even performed occasionally as a duo. Eastwood cut a couple of further singles and was part of a TV star compilation record, but his singing career went nowhere, not until *Paint Your Wagon* many years later. Still, Eastwood sings in a number of films; he would eventually compose music for his films and he would have a very profitable sideline in soundtracks from his later movies. But, bored with *Rawhide*, unable to direct and aware he'd never be a hit singer, he was open to new ideas. As it happens, his career was about to be transformed from an unlikely source.

Sergio Leone

Eastwood wasn't Sergio Leone's first choice to star in a Western he called *The Magnificent Stranger*. Leone passed on Richard Harrison, already a star in Italian sword-and-sandal epics, wanting instead Henry Fonda, but Fonda's agent refused to even submit the script to the actor. Leone probably offered it to Rory Calhoun, who had starred in his first film, *Colossus Of Rhodes*. He approached Charles Bronson, who turned him down flat, and James Coburn, who agreed to play the part but wanted $25,000, which was more than Leone's producers could afford. Fonda, Bronson and Coburn all wound up starring in later Leone Westerns.

Harrison apparently recommended Clint. Or maybe it was the William Morris agency in Rome. Or perhaps Ruth Marsh, Eastwood's original publicity agent. Lots of people want credit for bringing the two together. Some sources even suggest it was Eric Fleming, who was first offered the role. Certainly, the Morris agency also put it before Henry Silva.

Although he undoubtedly wanted a more experienced actor with a bigger box-office name, Leone was captivated immediately by the long, lean, animal laziness Clint exuded. When Clint got the script, his initial reaction was to immediately turn down an Italian Western but, as he read it, he recognised its source, Akira Kurosawa's film *Yojimbo* (itself a liberal adaptation of Dashiell Hammett's novel *Red Harvest*). Silva apparently held out for $16,000, but Clint, willing to visit Europe and keen to get away from *Rawhide*, agreed to the $15,000 fee budgeted.

A Fistful Of Dollars (1964)

Crew: Director: Sergio Leone, Producer: Harry Columbo/George Papi, Screenplay: Duccio Tessari, Victor A Catena, G Schock, Sergio Leone, based on *Yojimbo* by Akira Kurosawa and Ryuzo Kikushima, English Dialogue: Mark Lowell, Photography: Massimo Dallamano, Editor: Roberto Cinquini, Music: Ennio Morricone, Bruno Nicolai

Cast: Clint Eastwood (The Stranger), Gian Maria Volonte (Ramon Rojo), Marita Koch (Marisol), Wolfgang Lukschy (John Baxter)

Story: The Stranger (Joe) enters San Miguel, a border town controlled by two families, the Baxters and the Rojos. He successfully plays the two off against each other, then helps a woman escape from her life as a sex slave to Ramon Rojo. The Stranger is tortured, but his escape precipitates the massacre of the Baxters by the Rojos. Spirited out of town in a coffin, he recuperates in a cave. When he returns to save one of his benefactors, he kills the

Rojo gunmen. Knowing Ramon, an expert rifleman, will aim for his heart, The Stranger fashions a steel breastplate to deflect the bullets, and kills him

Transformation: Joe is figuratively reborn in the cave and returns to mete out vengeance.

Background: A Fistful Of Dollars established the screen character which has been the foundation of Eastwood's career ever since. The Man With No Name (originally a marketing concept) was a collaborative effort between Eastwood and Leone. Much of the costuming was Clint's, but the cigar and serape were touches added when the star arrived for filming in Spain. The combination of Leone's use of Clint's face and movement, and Clint's willingness to cut his own dialogue, resulted in an anti-hero unlike any that had been done before in Westerns. The film was an immediate hit in Italy, prompting a sequel. Eastwood had enjoyed the experience so much, he quickly agreed to reprise the role

Verdict: Arguably the key Western of the 1960s, and still fun. 4/5

For A Few Dollars More (1965)

Crew: Director: Sergio Leone, Producer: Alberto Grimaldi (PEA/Gonzalez/Constantin), Screenplay: Luciano Vincenzoni, Sergio Leone, Story: Fulvio Morsella, Sergio Leone, Photography: Massimo Dallamano, Editors: Eugenio Alabiso, Giorgio Serralonga, Music: Ennio Morricone

Cast: Clint Eastwood (Monco), Lee Van Cleef (Colonel Mortimer), Gian Maria Volonte (El Indio)

Story: Bounty killers Monco and Mortimer are both on the trail of escaped bandit Indio, a drug-addled psychopath. After a stand-off, they join forces, with Monco infiltrating Indio's gang and Mortimer lying in wait at the Bank of El Paso. After a successful robbery, Monco stays with Indio, while Mortimer shows up at the gang's rendezvous, offering his safe-breaking services. After being discovered and tortured, Indio sets them free so that they can eliminate Indio's gang. Indio gets the drop on Mortimer, only to be saved by Monco, who supervises a duel between the two using Mortimer's watch. The watch is the twin of Indio's – Indio's watch came from a woman who killed herself as he raped her. Mortimer kills Indio, revealing the woman was his sister. He tells Monco to keep the bounties and the reward for the bank's money.

Transformation: Interestingly, it is Mortimer who is transformed from bounty killer to moral avenger.

Background: Leone kept the three-way conflict of A Fistful Of Dollars, but refined it into three individuals and the result was a reduction of Eastwood's centrality. The film's main conflict is actually between Mortimer and Indio, with Monco literally playing referee and spectator at the end.

25

Eastwood's performance is pitched somewhere between Volonte's emotionalism and Van Cleef's reticence – it is as if the two poles of 1950s acting have been set there for Clint to bounce between. Yet, it is still Eastwood's presence which defines the film, and the lesson, that he could dominate the screen without necessarily dominating each scene, was not lost on him.

Verdict: Leone's small but perfectly-formed masterpiece 5/5

Clint's first two Spaghetti Westerns hadn't been released in the USA because Kurosawa sued over the rights to the *Yojimbo* story. Meanwhile, Vittorio De Sica offered Clint the chance to play in one of the five episodes of a portmanteau film designed to showcase De Sica's wife, Silvana Magnano. Clint was offered the choice of $25,000 or $20,000 plus a Ferrari – he took the latter option, figuring his agent couldn't take 10% of a Ferrari.

The Witches (1965)

(Part Five: A Night Like Any Other)
Crew: Director: Vittorio De Sica, Producer: Dino De Laurentiis, Screenplay: Cesare Zavattini, Fabio Carpi, Enzio Muzii, Photography: Giuseppe Rotunno, Editor: Adriana Novelli, Music: Pierto Piccinoi
Cast: Silvana Magnano (Giovanna), Clint Eastwood (Husband)
Background: De Sica's segment of this portmanteau is interesting, because it shows how quickly foreign film-makers recognised the essential elements in the characters of American stars. The film explores the fantasies of a bored housewife. Eastwood is the boring husband. He complains about the noise in Rome, he would rather sleep than make love and he would rather doze off than go see *A Fistful Of Dollars*. In her dreams, she recalls her wilder single life and transforms her husband into a dashing lover. She fantasizes about admiring men pursuing her up the Via Veneto, only to have them shot by her husband, now dressed in black (à la Jack Palance in *Shane*) in a Leone-like ritual setting. She then takes her clothes off to the delight of the male crowd, and the husband turns the gun on himself.

Eastwood's casting makes a specific connection between the buttoned-down, horn-rimmed American organisation man, as played by Rock Hudson, and his own cowboy heroes, implying the violence in the latter is the result of the sublimated sexuality of the former. De Sica put Clint in horn-rims to narrow the distance between The Man With No Name and the American hero who had chastely courted Doris Day.

Verdict: Don't confuse theoretically interesting with entertaining. 1/5

The Good, The Bad And The Ugly (1966)

Crew: Director: Sergio Leone, Producer: Alberto Grimaldi (PEA/United Artists), Screenplay: Age Scarpelli (Agenore Incrocci and Furio Scarpelli), Luciano Vincenzoni, Sergio Leone, Sergio Donati, Story: Luciano Vincenzoni, Sergio Leone, English Dialogue: Mickey Knox, Photography: Tonino Delli Colli, Editors: Nino Baragli, Eugenio Alabiso, Music: Ennio Morricone

Cast: Clint Eastwood (Blondie), Lee Van Cleef (Angel Eyes), Eli Wallach (Tuco)

Story: Texas during the Civil War. Angel Eyes is hunting down Jackson, responsible for stealing a shipment of Confederate gold. Blondie and Tuco have fallen out after working a scam where the former turns in the latter for reward, then shoots him free of the noose. Tuco has the upper hand when they come upon a dying Jackson, and each learns a part of the secret of the buried gold. When the two are captured by Union troops, they discover Angel Eyes running the prison camp. He tortures Tuco to learn the location of the gold, but offers Blondie a partnership. Tuco escapes and rejoins Blondie. On their way to the cemetery where the gold is hidden, they join a futile Union attack on a bridge. Blondie aids a dying Confederate soldier, and exchanges his duster for the soldier's poncho. In the cemetery, a three-way duel leaves Angel Eyes dead. Blondie makes Tuco dig up the gold, then strings him up and leaves him balancing on a graveyard cross. Disappearing over a hill, Blondie shoots Tuco's noose away one last time.

Transformation: The poncho from the dead soldier turns Blondie into The Man With No Name, and, from that point, he is in control of the action.

Background: With Eli Wallach taking Volonte's over-the-top role and Lee Van Cleef refining his look of leering evil, Eastwood's presence was once again dominant without ever being the central focus of the film. At least, not until the transformation scenes at the very end. Leone was learning to transform his films into epics, and Eastwood obviously paid attention.

Clint refused Leone's offer to reprise his role one last time. Leone intended to kill off the three characters at the opening of *Once Upon A Time In The West*. Wallach and Van Cleef had agreed, but Eastwood said no. As it happens, the opening of that film turned out to be one of the greatest in cinema.

Verdict: The ultimate pulp epic. 5/5

Malpaso

Leone's Spaghetti Westerns transformed Clint into a bankable star. There was an element of luck in this. The legal problems involving Kurosawa and the rights to his *Yojimbo* script meant that United Artists waited until the dispute was settled, then released the Dollars trilogy in America over an eleven-month period in 1967-68. Their reputation built by word of mouth and, with each film's increasing style, better casts and higher level of excitement, turned Clint into a major star almost overnight. Suddenly, he was in demand. So what does Clint do? He sets up Malpaso and pursues two careers simultaneously. One as a studio head and director. The other as an action star for hire.

Eastwood's business manager, Irving Leonard, was placed in charge of Malpaso. Leonard, who was very effective in getting Clint the control he wanted, died in 1969, only 53. (Robert Daley, an old friend of Eastwood's and a successful television producer, took his place.) Eastwood's agents, William Morris, were looking for him to take higher-profile projects (like *McKenna's Gold*), but he opted first for a Leone-esque Western script by Leonard Freeman and Mel Goldberg. His deal, set up through his new production company, called for $400,000, 25% of the net returns and a bigger cut of Italian takings, which virtually guaranteed him major money. Although veteran Western directors Robert Aldrich and John Sturges were considered to direct, Eastwood insisted on Ted Post. They had worked together on *Rawhide* and Eastwood felt comfortable with him.

Hang 'Em High (1968)

Crew: Director: Ted Post, Producer: Leonard Freeman (United Artists/Malpaso), Screenplay: Leonard Freeman, Mel Goldberg, Photography: Richard Kline, Lennie South, Editor: Gene Fowler Jr., Music: Dominic Frontiere

Cast: Clint Eastwood (Jed Cooper), Pat Hingle (Judge Fenton), Ed Begley (Captain Wilson), Inger Stevens (Rachel), Arlene Golonka (Jennifer), James MacArthur (Priest), Bruce Dern (Miller), Ben Johnson (Bliss), Dennis Hopper (Prophet), LQ Jones, Alan Hale Jr, Bob Steele, Ruth White

Story: Captain Wilson and his men hang Jed Cooper for rustling their cattle, though Cooper bought the herd legitimately from the actual rustlers. Cooper survives the hanging, is brought to town in a paddy wagon and is cleared by Judge Fenton. The Judge hires Cooper as a marshal, with the proviso that Cooper will not take the law into his own hands. Cooper brings in prisoners but questions Fenton's relish for hanging, particularly when two youngsters are hung. He also learns about vengeance from Rachel, who searches each load of prisoners for the men who killed her husband and raped her. When Wilson ambushes Cooper in a bar, Rachel nurses him back to health. Cooper hunts down Wilson's men, killing them off one by one, and Wilson finally hangs himself. Cooper tries to quit but Fenton persuades him to stay on as a marshal.

Transformation: Rancher Cooper is reborn, almost literally, as a lawman.

Background: This attempt to place the Leone hero into an American context raises far more questions than it answers, but was more successful at the American box office than any of Leone's films. It became United Artists' biggest hit of the year, bigger than James Bond, and probably taught Eastwood his first lesson about the value of worrying about subtlety. Many of the beatings and killings are over the top, almost cartoonish. The film plays like a Spaghetti Western with a movie-of-the-week debate on capital punishment thrown in. In fact, many of the people we see hung or killed are not villains at all. A more carefully thought-out film would raise serious questions about the nature of the lone vigilante, but *Hang 'Em High* never allows itself that luxury, though it does provide an interesting little foretaste of *Dirty Harry*.

Clint also began to learn how to deal with producers – at one point he banned Freeman from the set. Ted Post's direction is rarely better than straightforward and shows the influence of television practices. For example, where Leone inserts close-ups for effect, whilst Post cuts between them to show you who is talking.

The role of Inger Stevens as Rachel is a promising one, suggestive of the female parts in *High Plains Drifter* or *Pale Rider*, but she gets precious little space to do anything with it. Like Clint, Stevens had graduated from television, like Jean Seberg she would commit suicide.

Verdict: A disappointment after the Leone Westerns. 2/5

Don Siegel

The partnership with Sergio Leone may have been the most crucial in providing Clint with both a career breakthrough and an enduring on-screen persona, but Don Siegel is the biggest influence on Eastwood's directing career and was the director with whom he maintained the longer creative working partnership.

Siegel was a long-time Hollywood professional who was fiercely independent in his views but could get along with people. Never as iconoclastic as say Sam Fuller, his films are characterised by a narrative drive and his 1950s work, particularly *Invasion Of The Body Snatchers*, *The Line-up*, *Riot In Cell Block 11* and *Baby Face Nelson*, proved he could make the most of B-movie budgets and conditions. More importantly, Siegel's films focused on lone, often chaotic, individuals in conflict with the demands of a conformist society. These are iconoclasts who can't function under authority's yoke (much like Siegel himself within the studio system). The quintessential Siegel hero is Charley Varrick, billed as 'The Last of The Independents' in the eponymous film.

Siegel's films are even more overpoweringly masculine than Leone's. Where Leone had only a few, largely symbolic, roles for women, in Siegel's films women are invariably revealed to be evil and destroyers of men. Even 'good' women are subject to raging emotions which render them dangerous. For a male loner, this is a perilous kind of world.

Siegel may have hated producers, but he could work with star performers. His *Flaming Star* was one of the two or three films to successfully integrate Elvis Presley into a movie. On the surface, Siegel was a perfect match for Eastwood, whose character had already been established as an outsider, if not a rebel, and whose star qualities were beginning to be recognised. Already under contract at Universal, Siegel was brought in late to Eastwood's next project, replacing the original director, Alex Segal. At the time, neither he nor Clint knew of each other…

Coogan's Bluff (1968)

Crew: Director: Don Siegel, Executive Producer: Richard Lyons, Producer: Siegel (Universal), Screenplay: Herman Miller, Dean Reisner, Howard Rodman, (Uncredited: Roland Kibbe, Jack Laird), Story: Miller, Photography: Bud Thackery, Editor: Sam Waxman, Music: Lalo Schifrin

Cast: Clint Eastwood (Walt Coogan), Lee J Cobb (McElroy), Susan Clark (Julie), Tisha Sterling (Linny Raven), Don Stroud (Ringerman), Melodie Johnson, Albert Popwell, Seymour Cassell, Tom Tully

Story: Maverick Arizona cop Coogan is sent to New York to bring back a prisoner Ringerman, a man he'd once tracked and captured. Running into apathy and bureaucracy, and unable to make instant headway with social worker Julie, Coogan bluffs his way into getting Ringerman released into his custody, only to be ambushed on his way to the helicopter. He starts tracking his man through the urban wasteland of New York by tracing his hippie girlfriend Linny. After sleeping with her, she leads him into a trap. When an irate Julie learns from Linny that Coogan seduced her, she shows up at his room, incensed. Coogan threatens Linny with violence, and she leads him to Ringerman, hiding out at the Cloisters. A motorcycle chase later, Coogan captures his prey. Returning to Arizona, he is seen off by Julie.

Transformation: Coogan turns from cowboy sheriff into city cop

Background: With this film, Clint's cowboy persona becomes a detective. By setting him in the urban backdrop of New York, Siegel paved the way for the *Dirty Harry* series (not to mention the TV show *McCloud*).

Siegel's opening shots clearly echo Leone's desert panoramas, and the fugitive Indian stripped to his loincloth evokes the close proximity of the Wild West. The Man With No Name becomes a modern cowboy cop, and a recognisable American hero.

In New York, however, Siegel effects an even more important transformation. Lee J Cobb's McElroy is a tired cop right out of Siegel's previous police thriller *Madigan* (which also featured Clark and Stroud), and Eastwood as Coogan injects US Grade A prime heroic energy into the detective. This sparked off an entire cycle of cop movies, including *Dirty Harry*, where a new vigorous approach to crime-fighting replaced the tired old liberal clichés which grew out of the Film Noir era.

It almost didn't happen. Siegel and Eastwood came to the film with different versions of the script, which went through many writers. Eventually, the two men cut and pasted the drafts together and then brought Dean Reisner in to polish the resulting script.

Clint's love scenes had been left on the cutting room floor in Leone's Westerns, but now he got the chance to indulge himself. Coogan adapted happily to Siegel's deeply misogynistic world, and his relationships with women would begin to define the four broad categories described earlier. Coogan gets sent to New York because his chief catches him trysting with a married woman when he should be delivering a prisoner; the woman demonstrates no guilt at being caught in the act (Whore). Coogan's country charm is slow to work on the briskly efficient Julie but, when she discovers he's slept with Linny, she attacks Coogan in a fit of jealousy (Working Wannabe). By the movie's end, Julie is presented as a waif, waving helplessly as Coogan leaves her behind (and he shares a smoke with his curiously feminine prisoner). Finally, the seemingly waif-like flower child Linny turns out to be a sadistic whore, happy to make love to Coogan and then set him up for a fierce beating.

Verdict: Siegel's pace suits the film and you can see he's looking for the right counterpoint to Clint's star presence. A key transition work for both Clint and the genre. 4/5

This Gun For Hire

Soon after *Coogan's Bluff* wrapped, Eastwood acted in four major projects which banked on his established image as a cowboy and a cold killer. The fees available ($850,000 for *Where Eagles Dare*, $500,000 plus points for *Paint Your Wagon*) induced him to follow what was the recognised path for a big star, and his next film paired him with one of the giants, Richard Burton.

Where Eagles Dare (1968)

Crew: Director: Brian G Hutton, Producer: Elliott Kastner (MGM), Screenplay: Alistair MacLean, Photography: Arthur Ibbetson, Editor: John Jympson, Music: Ron Goodwin, Art Director: Peter Mullins, Second Unit Director/Stunts: Yakima Canutt

Cast: Richard Burton (Major John Smith), Clint Eastwood (Lt. Morris Schaffer), Mary Ure (Mary Ellison), Anton Diffring (Colonel Kramer), Derren Nesbit (Major Von Hapen), Ferdy Mayne (Rosemeyer), Michael Hordern (Admiral Rolland), Patrick Wymark (Colonel Turner), Ingrid Pitt (Heidi), Robert Beatty (General Carnaby)

Story: A Commando team, headed by Major Smith, parachutes in behind German lines to free US General Carnaby from a German castle on a mountaintop. The team includes American Schaffer, and the mission turns out to be a ruse designed to expose the identity of German spies within British intelligence. As an outsider, Schaffer is the only person Smith can trust. After a harrowing battle, they escape and are rescued. The top German agent is exposed and kills himself.

Background: Eastwood says his role in this film was to look puzzled and kill people, not necessarily in that order. It's still fun to wonder why he doesn't kill the radio operator with his silenced pistol, rather than creeping up and giving him the chance to sound an alarm. But, of course, by doing it that way he creates the opportunity for a large-scale Kraut harvest, including the famous two sub-machine gun mow-down. This picture was a chance for Burton to reclaim his international star status without working alongside his wife, Elizabeth Taylor, and, as an A-project, he and Eastwood would benefit by each other's presence and audience draw. Eastwood got on famously with the world's most famous acting couple and nearly worked with Taylor soon after, before she backed out of *Two Mules For Sister Sara*.

The main stunt work was done by Yakima Canutt, who had done the chariot races for both versions of *Ben-Hur*, working with Sergio Leone on the remake, and had doubled for John Wayne in *Stagecoach*.

Verdict: It is what it is – one of the ultimate Boy's Own movies. Still fun to watch. 3/5

Paint Your Wagon (1969)

Crew: Director: Joshua Logan, Producer: Alan Jay Lerner (Paramount), Screenplay: Alan Jay Lerner, Play: Alan Jay Lerner, Frederick Loewe, Adaptation: Paddy Chayefsky, Photography: William Fraker, Editor: Robert Jones, Music: Frederick Loewe, Additional Songs: André Prévin, Musical Director: Nelson Riddle, Production Design: John Truscott

Cast: Lee Marvin (Ben), Clint Eastwood (Pardner), Jean Seberg (Elizabeth), Harve Presnell (Rotten Luck Willie), Ray Walston (Mad Jack Duncan), Tom Ligon (Horton Fenty), Alan Dexter (Parson), John Mitchum (Jacob Woodling)

Story: Ben and Pardner are partners because Ben struck gold in what was intended to be Pardner's brother's grave. Womanless, Ben buys Elizabeth from Jacob Woodling, a Mormon with two wives. When Ben agrees to hijack a wagonload of French ladies for his fellow miners, Elizabeth and Pardner fall in love. Elizabeth overcomes Ben's jealous rage by suggesting a Mormon-style ménage-à-trois but, when the respectable Fentys arrive in town, Ben gets booted out of the ménage. He begins tunnelling under the town's saloons, trying to recover gold dust which has fallen through the cracks in the floors. Eventually, the town collapses, Ben and the majority of miners leave, while Elizabeth and Pardner stay behind.

Background: The biggest impact *Paint Your Wagon* had on Eastwood's career was the experience of watching director Josh Logan's film spin out of control. He also discovered once and for all how much he hated waiting around on set doing nothing.

The idea was Marvin would reprise his Oscar-winning *Cat Ballou* role, Eastwood would play The Man With No Voice and Logan would work his magic on a story which is *Camelot*'s love triangle transposed to the Old West. The chance to resume singing was a major attraction for Eastwood. It may have sounded good on paper, but the result was a film massively over schedule and budget that played like a series of tableaux barely vivants.

Clint's singing doesn't grate. Lee Marvin's does on one song and doesn't on the other. Jean Seberg makes an appealing waif, who turns out to be a very practical woman indeed (her songs, by the way, were the only ones dubbed). Clint later said he saw four different cuts of this film, and the best was the first, Logan's own. The fourth was the one released. It made lots of money.

Verdict: Watching it isn't always as bad as it sounds, but it ain't good. 2/5

Two Mules For Sister Sara (1970)

Crew: Director: Don Siegel, Producer: Martin Rackin/Carroll Case (Universal/Malpaso), Screenplay: Albert Maltz, Story: Budd Boetticher, Photography: Gabriel Figueroa, Editors: Robert Shugrue, Juan Jose Marino, Music: Ennio Morricone, Art Director: Jose Rodriguez Granada, Camera Operator: Bruce Surtees, Stunts: Wayne "Buddy" Van Horn

Cast: Clint Eastwood (Hogan), Shirley MacLaine (Sara), Manolo Fabregas (Colonel Beltran), Alberto Morin (Général Le Claire)

Story: Mercenary Hogan is on his way to join Mexican revolutionaries in an attack on the French fort at Chihuahua (in return for half the French gold) when he rescues a naked woman from three men trying to rape her. She turns out to be a nun being pursued by the French because of her sympathy for the revolutionaries. Hogan lets her accompany him. She saves his life and Hogan starts to find her increasingly attractive. When they reach Chihuahua, she turns out to be a local whore, abused by the French. By turning her in to the French, Hogan infiltrates the fort, the revolutionaries capture it, Hogan gets his share of the gold and goes off with his nun.

Transformation: MacLaine's character is reborn, from nun to whore and from revolutionary (i.e. 'feminist') to Hogan's 'pardner.' Read into that what you will.

Background: If, on the surface, Clint may have felt happy to rebound from the chaos of *Paint Your Wagon* to the friendlier confines of a Siegel set, this was not a typical Eastwood/Siegel collaboration. The project was intended for Eastwood and Liz Taylor, but Taylor preferred to stay in Europe with Burton and MacLaine, who at the time was Hollywood's first choice for any whore-with-a-heart-of-gold role, seemed a reasonable replacement. It required some character changes (she couldn't play Mexican) and she soon clashed with both Siegel and Eastwood. Siegel's analysis – "She's too unfeminine… she has too much balls. She's very hard." – is revealing. Siegel and Eastwood's habit of intimidating actresses who gave them trouble, like Susan Clark, didn't get far with MacLaine.

More importantly, Siegel clashed from the start with producer Rackin, who retained final cut of the film (though Siegel tried not to shoot enough coverage to make many changes). Rackin had bought the original screenplay from Budd Boetticher, then hired Albert Maltz to rewrite it. The original story predates the run of ostensibly political Spaghetti Westerns which teamed gringo mercenaries with Mexican revolutionaries or bandits but, by the time they got to shoot the film, most of the issues had been eliminated and what was left was something closer to a man/woman version of the Blondie/Tuco bounty relationship. Intended as a Mexican *African Queen* or *Heaven Knows Mr Allison*, it has little of the wit of those films. This is mostly because, right from the start, MacLaine's character appears to be motivated more by a whore's instinct than by a nun's. Her broad playing and mugging behind Hogan's back undercut the whole idea that she is what she appears to be. And neither Siegel nor Eastwood appear to be ready to allow MacLaine the space to play as a revolutionary equal; it's as if the audience is waiting for the moment when she will collapse and confirm that she is a mere waif after all. The interplay between the two leads is entertaining, but Eastwood's restraint when playing a similar situation (wounded man at the mercy of a woman) in *The Beguiled* is far more successful.

It's significant that after this film Clint didn't work with a major female star until Meryl Streep in *The Bridges Of Madison County*. He later played alongside some very talented actresses with lesser star status, like Jessica Walter or most notably Geneviève Bujold, and had lesser roles for excellent character actresses, like Carrie Snodgress and Verna Bloom. In fairness, he wouldn't share the screen with many major male stars either, until Burt Reynolds in *City Heat*. Eastwood's star persona and acting style were built around him dominating the screen, and his approach as a director was to play his persona off skilled character actors. At its best, it provides fine work for character actors. At its worst, it is almost cartoonish, as we see when those actors play second fiddle to an ape.

Verdict: 2/5

Kelly's Heroes (1970)

Crew: Director: Brian G Hutton, Producers: Gabriel Katzka, Sidney Beckerman (MGM), Screenplay: Troy Kennedy Martin, Photography: Gabriel Figueroa, Editor: John Jympson, Music: Lalo Schifrin, Art Director: Jonathan Barry, Second Unit Director: Andrew Marton

Cast: Clint Eastwood (Kelly), Telly Savalas (Big Joe), Donald Sutherland (Oddball), Don Rickles (Crapgame), Caroll O'Connor (General Colt),

Gaven MacLeod (Moriarty), Fred Pearlman (Mitchell), George Savalas (Mulligan), Stuart Margolin (Little Joe)

Story: While trying to learn the location of brothels from a captured German colonel, Kelly discovers the existence of 14,000 bars of gold and decides to steal it. He assembles a team including wheeler-dealer supply sergeant Crapgame and freelance tank commander Oddball. As they move toward their objective, General Colt assumes they are leading an attack. Kelly's men take the town and make a deal with the last German tank commander to share the gold, just as Colt and his troops arrive in town.

Background: As with *Paint Your Wagon*, Eastwood learned what happens when a production loses control. What started as a sharp antiwar comedy wound up as a terribly uneven, unfocused and uncomfortable hybrid after the studio bosses got their hands on the footage. In many ways, the film's message was ahead of its time – it prefigured *M*A*S*H* – but the intent was soon lost in a mishmash of genres: caper movie, war movie, parody Western and satire.

Verdict: 2/5

After hiring himself out for big money on three 'prestige' pictures, Eastwood had learned some important lessons. He had been appalled at the waste which bad planning and Hollywood profligacy could bring. He developed a wariness for big stars and the demands which sometimes went along with their status. And he saw what could happen when a director, even one as talented as Siegel, had no control over the finished product.

Not only would studios damage a finished film, they could also take steps to ensure its failure. *Two Mules For Sister Sara* and *Kelly's Heroes* were released virtually at the same time, ensuring neither would do well. Together their box office would be less than half of *Paint Your Wagon*'s, which was still running when the other two opened and closed quickly in the summer of 1970. Eastwood's quest for control of his own projects can certainly be dated from this time.

By contrast, working with Siegel was a marriage of minds: Siegel deplored waste, knew what he wanted and how to get it, and trusted his creative team. Siegel also recognised what star presence he had in Eastwood and what values he could bring to the production side of a film. Siegel was a savvy enough operator to defer to his star, while being a confident and efficient enough director to produce coherent results. By now the partnership was more a full-scale relationship, right down to their pet names for each other, Clintus and Siegelini.

First Cycle: Clintus & Siegelini
(& John Sturges)

I've divided Clint's career into four cycles, each of which ends with a western which serves to consolidate the cycle's films. To me, *Hang 'Em High* and *Coogan's Bluff* are part of his first cycle, while *Two Mules For Sister Sara* is not. None of the preceding four films were projects whose finished success or failure reflected Clint's creative input, and on *Two Mules For Sister Sara* even Siegel's input was restrained. The real effect of those four films was to increase Clint's leverage at the box office, and even that was threatened by the clumsy release of the last two. From now on, Eastwood would control his on-screen image. As it evolved, so did he. He began his career as a director with a short documentary about the shooting of his next film. He directed and presented the film, about Don Siegel directing him in a gothic tale...

The Beguiled (1971)

Crew: Director: Don Siegel, Producer: Don Siegel (Universal/Malpaso), Screenplay: John B Sherry (Albert Maltz), Grimes Grice (Irene Kamp) (and Claude Traverse, credited as Associate Producer), Novel: Thomas Cullinan, Photography: Bruce Surtees, Editor: Carl Pingitore, Music: Lalo Schifrin, Production Design: Ted Haworth, Art Director: Alexander Golitzen

Cast: Clint Eastwood (John McBurney), Geraldine Page (Martha), Elizabeth Hartman (Edwina), JoAnn Harris (Carol), Pamelyn Ferdin (Amy), Mae Mercer (Hallie), Darlene Carr (Doris), Melody Thomas (Abagail)

Story: Union corporal McBurney, wounded badly, is discovered by mushroom-picking 12-year-old Amy. Taken back to her school full of Southern women, "McB" in turn charms spinster teacher Edwina, the owner Miss Martha (whose great love was an incestuous affair with her brother, and who harbours longings for Edwina) and the slave Hallie (who was raped by Martha's brother). Though most of the students hate him as the enemy, 17-year-old Carol makes her desire plain. One night, McB climbs the stairs, pausing to decide whether to visit Martha or Edwina, both of whom are waiting. Carol pre-empts his choice by luring him to her room, but she makes noises and they are discovered. The wounded McB is knocked down the stairs. His leg is severely broken and the women amputate it. The loss of his leg maddens him – whilst drunk, he reveals secrets about the women and kills Amy's pet turtle. Although Edwina's declarations of love calm him down, the other women fear what he may do and decide to kill him. At dinner, McB apologises and announces he and

Edwina will be leaving to get married, but he has already been poisoned with mushrooms picked by Amy...

Transformation: As McB is transformed from beguiler to beguiled, he is also transformed from soldier to corpse.

Background: Although the beguiled of the title are clearly intended to be the women, in the end McB becomes the beguiled, falling prey to the foolish notion that, as a man, he is somehow in control of the situation. He says, "I sure thank Providence for sending me here," but as we all know, the Lord sometimes works in mysterious ways. Although he beguiles the women and girls one by one, he releases the dangerous spectre of sexuality into the equation and transforms a situation he understands (the all-male world of war) into one he doesn't (the all-female world of emotions, which is more dangerous).

As Siegel explained in a letter to Eastwood (quoted by Stuart Kaminsky): 'behind the facade of innocent faces... lurks just as much evil as in a group of hoodlums.' McB will not be the first character in Eastwood's oeuvre killed for stepping over the bounds of sexuality. (Compare these schoolgirls to the whores in *Unforgiven*.)

Universal Studios' Jennings Lang would later attribute *The Beguiled*'s failure at the box office to the idea that "people didn't want to see Clint Eastwood lose a leg." The lesson was not lost on Eastwood and his character has only died in one other film, *Honkytonk Man*, and he did that over the studio's objections.

Verdict: This remains one of Siegel and Eastwood's finest films. 5/5

Play Misty For Me (1971)

Crew: Director: Clint Eastwood, Producer: Robert Daley (Universal/ Malpaso), Screenplay: Jo Heims, Dean Reisner, Photography: Bruce Surtees, Editor: Carl Pingitore, Music: Dee Barton, Art Director: Alexander Golitzen

Cast: Clint Eastwood (Dave Garver), Jessica Walter (Evelyn Draper), Donna Mills (Tobie), Don Siegel (Murphy), John Larch (Sgt. McCallum), James McEachin (Al Monte), George Fargo, Jack Kosslyn

Story: Carmel, California, DJ Dave Garver picks up Evelyn in a bar, but discovers she has engineered the meeting and is the woman who calls his show regularly, asking him to play 'Misty' for her. Evelyn professes to have a liberal, casual attitude toward sex, but becomes increasingly possessive. Dave's true love, Tobie, returns after three months of trying to rationalise Dave's wayward nature with his professed love for her. Dave indicates his desire to change and declares his love for Tobie. As a result, Evelyn makes a public scene which ruins Dave's chance for a big job, then she attempts suicide, tears Dave's apartment apart and attacks his housekeeper. Released on bail, Evelyn becomes Tobie's roommate, holding her hostage, killing a police sergeant and finally attacking Dave with a knife. She slashes him repeatedly before he punches her through a window and over his balcony to her death on the rocks below.

Transformation: Dave is transformed from tomcat to loyal heroic boyfriend (maybe).

Background: Eastwood offered to make this film so cheaply and quickly that the studio had nothing to lose by letting him go ahead. He optioned the story from Jo Heims, whom he'd known as a secretary, but couldn't get anyone interested in financing the film and was worried about entrusting it to any director but the unavailable Siegel. By waiving a director's fee, Eastwood made the film for less than $750,000, which was a bargain even in those days.

It is a key work in his career and an outstanding first feature. The finished product was probably a surprise to almost everyone because Eastwood showed a very sure directing touch and produced a film which, despite a couple of longueurs, holds up better than its unofficial remake, *Fatal Attraction*. (Eastwood famously told studio boss Sherry Lansing she owed him a beer for stealing his story.)

From the opening helicopter shots of the coastline, the visual sense is both attractive and integrated into the storytelling, a point made even clearer by an impressive audio link from silence to seagulls to Dave's radio show. Eastwood chose familiar territory and saved money by shooting on location, but he was also aware of the impact the jagged, beautiful but threatening Northern California coastline could have on the mood of his film. The idyllic exteriors also reflected Garver's equally idyllic masculine world and contrasted with the ever-increasing darkness which eventually takes over the film.

In that sense, *Play Misty For Me* makes the transition from relationship film to horror picture far more convincingly than *Fatal Attraction*, and it's interesting to watch the moving camera elements which follow on from *The Beguiled*. In many ways, *Play Misty For Me* is a Siegel-style film, a fact signalled by Siegel's key role as bartender Murphy, but it moves on from his vein of misogyny. Cry Bastard, the game Siegel and Eastwood use to entice Walter over, is a male in-joke, a coded ritual which, it turns out, is used by Walter for her own purposes. This signals that she may be both dangerous and deadly. (The game recalls Tegwar, 'the exciting game without any rules' in Mark Harris' novel and John Hancock's film *Bang The Drum Slowly*). Relationships, in the Siegel/Eastwood world, are just like that game.

Play Misty For Me is often accused of being a Neanderthal reaction to the growing threat of woman's liberation to macho prerogatives, but that misreads Evelyn's basic hang-up. When Dave accepts casual sex, but insists on retaining the traditional masculine imperative to initiate contact (a role which she has reversed by choreographing her own pick-up), Evelyn reacts by becoming a clinging, baby-talking, stuffed-animal holding, dependent woman – her collapse into psychopathy is a result of her inability to assert a liberated response to Dave, and rather slipping back into a traditional woman's role.

Meanwhile, Tobie (the Californian blonde) is trying to decide whether Dave's wanderings are worth putting up with. Tobie is problematic, and not just because the extended *Elvira Madigan*-style love scene set to a Roberta Flack song grated then and grates even worse now. She is, on the surface, more liberated (she works, which Evelyn doesn't seem to do), but she wants a traditional commitment from Dave. In the end, she becomes the very traditional damsel in distress. For some reason Evelyn doesn't kill Tobie, but she does get to deliver the film's best line. As Tobie finally realises who her roommate is, Evelyn says, "God you're dumb," and we tend to agree.

Garver's future problems are predicted when Al Monte asks Garver why he would fool around when Tobie is so fine. Garver says, "it's just a hang-up I have," to which Al replies, "He who lives by the sword shall die by the sword." Dave's relationship with Al is the first of many instances of Eastwood's personal commitment to multiracial casting. Al is also one of Clint's few black partners to make it through to the last reel in one piece. The scenes at the Monterey Festival, where they go on a mixed-race double date, show two multiracial bands, the Johnny Otis Show and Cannonball Adderly's Quintet.

Verdict: Despite that awful love sequence, *Play Misty For Me* holds up as a thriller. 4/5

Warner Brothers executive Frank Wells, who had been Clint's lawyer, lured him to Warner Brothers for his next film, which had started life as a Frank Sinatra project. Don Siegel came on loan from Universal, as did Dean Reisner, who polished a script that had gone through many writers. The result was the mainstream breakthrough film that created Eastwood's urban personality. (Sinatra would eventually do his own Harry in *The First Deadly Sin*.)

Dirty Harry (1971)

Crew: Director: Don Siegel, Executive Producer: Robert Daley, Producer: Don Siegel (Warner Brothers/Malpaso), Story: Harry Julian Fink, Rita M Fink, Screenplay: Harry Julian Fink, Rita M Fink, Dean Reisner (Uncredited: John Milius), Photography: Bruce Surtees, Editor: Carl Pingitore, Music: Lalo Schifrin, Art Director: Dale Hennessy, Stunts: Van Horn, Assistant To The Producer: George Fargo

Cast: Clint Eastwood (Harry Callahan), Harry Guardino (Lt. Bressler), Reni Santoni (Chico), John Vernon (Mayor), Andy Robinson (Scorpio), John Larch (Chief), John Mitchum (Frank DiGeorgio), Ruth Kobart (Bus Driver), Albert Popwell (Robber), Mae Mercer (Mrs Russell), Woodrow Parfey, Jo de Winter

Story: A killer named Scorpio is terrorising San Francisco. He takes a young girl hostage and demands a ransom from the city to reveal where she has been buried alive. Inspector "Dirty" Harry Callahan volunteers to deliver the ransom. He chases down Scorpio in Kezar Stadium, wounds him and tortures him into revealing the location of the girl, who is already dead. Scorpio is released because Harry violated his rights. Harry stalks him on his own time. Scorpio hires his own beating from a thug, then publicly blames Harry, who is suspended. Scorpio kidnaps a school bus, and asks for a ransom and an airplane. Harry intercepts the bus, chases Scorpio and kills him. He tosses away his badge.

Transformation: Harry is transformed from cop to ex-cop (until the first sequel).

Background: Still one of the most important police movies of all time, this was also the film which cemented Clint's anti-hero image in the eyes of America. The hysterical reaction of critics, led by Pauline Kael, accusing the film of fascism, is accepted as far-fetched today but seemed just as off-beat to some of us at the time. Even then, it was obvious they were missing the boat, perhaps as a knee-jerk reflex because the positive reaction from Middle America was so strong.

The film made clear Harry took people on their own merits, a fact hammered home by the scene with a black doctor. Harry is thick skinned enough to survive being called "Dirty" (he would become rather less dirty in each sequel) but others are more sensitive. In fact, it is Scorpio who is the racist, threatening "Catholics and niggers."

Harry's battle with Scorpio is often viewed as the silent majority's revenge on hippies, but it is crucial to remember that Scorpio's peace-symbol belt buckle is twisted and distorted, like his personality. The real battle is between Harry and the schmucks of bureaucracy. The real power lies not in the .44 Magnum or the car crashes, but in Harry's willingness to go it alone. It's easy to see every city government or chain of command as a symbol for a Hollywood studio.

Clint actually directed some second unit on this film, and the scenes where Harry talks a jumper off the roof (the potential suicide was played by Buddy Van Horn).

Verdict: Deservedly a classic, and just as sharp now as it was then. 5/5

Joe Kidd (1972)

Crew: Director: John Sturges, Executive Producer: Robert Daley, Producer: Sidney Beckerman (Universal/Malpaso), Screenplay: Elmore Leonard, Photography: Bruce Surtees, Editor: Ferris Webster, Music: Lalo Schifrin, Art Director: Alexander Golitzen, Henry Bumstead, Stunts: Buddy Van Horn, Assistant Director: James Fargo

Cast: Clint Eastwood (Joe Kidd), Robert Duvall (Frank Harlan), John Saxon (Luis Chama), Don Stroud (Lamar), James Wainwright (Mingo), Stella Garcia (Helen Sanchez), Paul Koslo (Roy), Gregory Walcott (Sheriff Mitchell), Lynne Marta (Elma), Dick Van Patten (Hotel Manager), John Carter (Judge), Ron Soble (Ramon)

Story: As New Mexico rancher Joe Kidd is being fined for disorderly conduct and hunting on Indian land, the courtroom is raided by Luis Chama on behalf of Mexicans whose lands are being stolen as a result of their Spanish deeds having been 'lost.' Land baron Harlan arrives in town with his gunmen, sporting the latest modern weaponry, and attempts to hire Kidd to track Chama down. Kidd refuses, but changes his mind after Chama's men steal his horses and abuse his ranch hand. Harlan kidnaps Helen, Chama's woman, and holds an entire village (and Kidd) hostage to lure Chama out. Kidd escapes, and discovers Chama is willing to let the villagers die to preserve his leadership. Kidd and Helen persuade Chama to give himself up to the law. Harlan lays an ambush in town, but Kidd overcomes it, kills Harlan and rides off with Helen.

Transformation: Joe is transformed from prisoner and outsider to lawman and family man (he 'brings in' Chama and gets his woman in the bargain).

Background: *Joe Kidd* is probably the most ignored crucial film of Clint's career. Henry Bumstead's design would prove essential to Clint's finest films. Bruce Surtees' photography reflects his father's work with John Sturges, and sets the tone for Eastwood's landscape shots in which large blocks of colour create an abstract look (one critic compared it to Rothko, but it seems closer to Californian artist Richard Diebenkorn). Joe Kidd could ride directly from this film into the landscape of *High Plains*

Drifter and never notice the difference. Compare the water in *High Plains Drifter* with the sky in this film, or Frank Stanley's photography in *Thunderbolt And Lightfoot*. Each film has isolated towns as small pockets of dirty chaos amidst the simple order of a natural landscape.

Joe Kidd also shows the conflict between an anti-hero and society's rules. In *A Fistful Of Dollars*, The Man With No Name played his own game using antagonism between the Baxters and the Rojos. However, Elmore Leonard's screenplay sets up a more political conflict, familiar from other Spaghetti Westerns, between the capitalist Harlan (whose name recalls the Harlan County wars) and the land-reform oriented revolutionary Chama.

When Joe is railroaded by a humiliated sheriff and the Mexicans are told by a powerless judge that their Spanish property deeds have been 'lost' in a fire, it's clear the law is not equivalent to justice in Sinola. Kidd's sympathies are obviously with Chama (he refuses Harlan's offer to hunt Chama down), but he changes his mind for personal reasons. Hunting Chama with Harlan, Kidd works against the implicit aim of the hunt. But having built audience sympathy for Chama and reinforced it by making Duvall's capitalist a potential mass murderer, the film then turns on Chama as well, drawing a parallel between him and Harlan. For some unexplained reason, Kidd the anti-hero suddenly becomes the upholder of order and Chama's woman, even more surprisingly, transfers her allegiance to Kidd and his plan for Chama to turn himself in. Chama appears to trust Kidd, even though he sets up Chama's lieutenant (the horse thief) for execution by Harlan's men. Suddenly, he has faith in gringo justice and doesn't even mind losing his woman to Kidd. Despite Kidd's victory in the final scene, sitting in the judge's chair to deal out justice (echoing the finale of *For A Few Dollars More*), we have no faith in Chama's future before the law.

If Helen Sanchez is a woman who is fit for a man of action, Harlan's mistress Elma, at first appears to be a whore open to Kidd's advances, then becomes a waif when Harlan calls her "Little Girl."

Verdict: *Joe Kidd* is nice to look at, but has huge holes. Lalo Schifrin's urban electric piano jars with the Morricone-style Duane Eddy-ish guitar. Director Sturges was very much on the downside physically, and it shows. I like it a lot, but it's not as good as it could have been. 3/5

High Plains Drifter (1973)

Crew: Director: Clint Eastwood, Executive Producer: Jennings Lang, Producer: Robert Daley (Universal/Malpaso), Screenplay: Ernest Tidyman, Photography: Bruce Surtees, Editor: Ferris Webster, Music: Dee Barton, Art Director: Henry Bumstead, Stunts: Buddy Van Horn

Cast: Clint Eastwood (The Stranger), Verna Bloom (Sarah Belding), Marianna Hill (Callie Travers), Mitchell Ryan (Dave Drake), Jack Ging (Morgan Allan), Stefan Giersach (Mayor), Ted Hartley (Lewis Belding), Billy Curtis (Mordecai), Geoffrey Lewis (Stacy Bridges), Scott Walker (Bill Borders), Walter Barnes (Sheriff), John Hillerman (Bootmaker), Robert Donner (Preacher), Richard Bull (Asa), Paul Brinegar (Lutie), Anthony James (Cole), William O'Connell (Barber), John Quade (Jake Ross), John Mitchum (Warden), Van Horn (Marshal Duncan)

Story: A Stranger rides into Lago, returning the unfriendly welcome by killing some predatory gunmen. When he ignores Callie's brazen approach, she becomes incensed. He rapes her in a barn, watched by Mordecai, a dwarf. Lago fears the revenge of the Bridges' gang, just released from prison, who once served the same function as the gunmen the Stranger just killed. In return for unlimited credit at the town's businesses, the Stranger agrees to stay. Through flashbacks, which may be the Stranger's nightmares, we see the Bridges gang whipping the town's former marshal to death while most of the town watches. The marshal is now buried in an unmarked grave.

The Stranger begins training the town to defend itself, commandeers goods, and tears down a barn to construct picnic tables. He has the town painted red and renames it Hell. The citizens try killing him, using Callie as the lure. He survives, accepts an increased bounty to stay and takes over the hotel (and the hotel keeper's wife). The wife and Mordecai are the only people not complicit in the marshal's death. She decides to leave her husband and the town. As Bridges' gang approaches, the Stranger leaves. The desperadoes discover Hell waiting with a "Welcome Home" banner. As they wreak their revenge, setting the town aflame, the Stranger returns, strangling one and hanging another with a whip. He guns down Bridges. In the morning he leaves the now-destroyed town. The Marshal now has a proper tombstone. "I never did know your name," says Mordecai. "Yes you do," the Stranger replies, and disappears into the distance.

Transformation: The Stranger is, literally or not, Marshall Jim Duncan reborn.

Background: It has been said that if *Play Misty For Me* is Clint's version of a Siegel film, then *High Plains Drifter* is his version of a Leone movie.

Though there is some truth in that view, Clint had already made substantial moves away from Leone and those differences are far more revealing than the similarities. The most important difference is the nature of the Stranger, who gets an objective correlative, as it were, in the murdered Jim Duncan. Apart from the one moment in *A Fistful Of Dollars* where Joe explains that once he knew someone like Marisol and there was no one there to help, there is never any moral motivation for Clint's character in Leone's films. However, Mortimer had a motive in *For A Few Dollars More*. Like him, the Stranger is seeking revenge for a specific act, which is shown in a dream or flashback.

The women in the film continue to break new ground from the Siegel paradigm. Callie is Linny Raven or Carol, but Verna Bloom's Sarah is a capable woman, stronger than her husband, confident in herself and her relation with the Stranger. She is a prototype for the Carrie Snodgress character in *Pale Rider*.

Verdict: Assured and mysterious, this is the work of a mature film-maker. 4/5

Second Cycle: The Limits Of Genre

With *Play Misty For Me* and *High Plains Drifter*, Clint had made one film which could be identified with each of his mentors. He was now, in effect, free to find his own voice and it's interesting that he started with another romance, like *Play Misty For Me*, scripted by Jo Heims with him in mind.

Breezy (1973)

Crew: Director: Clint Eastwood, Executive Producer: Jennings Lang, Producer: Robert Daley (Universal/Malpaso), Screenplay: Jo Heims, Photography: Frank Stanley, Editor: Ferris Webster, Music: Michel Legrand, Art Director: Alexander Golitzen

Cast: William Holden (Frank Harmon), Key Lenz (Breezy), Roger C Carmel (Bob Henderson), Joan Hotchkis (Paula Harmon), Marj Dusay (Betty Tobin), Norman Barthold, Jack Kosslyn, Scott Holden

Story: Disillusioned man in mid-life crisis meets hippie chick. Old man loses girl (age and culture clash lead him to give her up). Old man reconsiders (friend whose new husband is killed in a car crash shows him loneliness) and gets girl.

Transformation: Love allows bitter, frustrated Frank to become a groovy guy.

Background: As a tale of culture and consciousness clash, this is the kind of film which, in the hands of a Frank Perry, might have been seen as sharp social comment, but Eastwood leads it down a romantic blind alley. Part of the problem is that even though William Holden does a fine job of acting out Frank's rebirth as a person, it comes so quickly and he's so decent from the first, that we aren't quite sure why his life was such a failure.

This may be because without himself in the lead, Eastwood the director adds sentimentality. It's hard to see Eastwood the director letting Clint the actor utter some of Frank's speeches, which venture into internal sensitivity, and may be why Clint passed on the role in the first place. Where the romances and oppositions in *Play Misty For Me* and *High Plains Drifter* were straightforward (good woman/bad woman) and set in the context of a genre structure, *Breezy* lacks a rough-edged contrast. Without that structure and the depths it builds into characters, Eastwood might have had to reveal far more than he was willing to do. So Holden gets the task.

Note that *High Plains Drifter* is shown at the movies, and the director has a quick walk-on as a bystander.

Verdict: Soppy, but a surprisingly interesting actors' movie. 2/5

Eastwood was growing frustrated with Universal, who hadn't put much marketing muscle behind his first three directorial efforts. Warner Brothers, on the other hand, took the Dirty Harry franchise and ran...

Magnum Force (1973)

Crew: Director: Ted Post, Producer: Robert Daley (Warner Brothers/ Malpaso), Screenplay: John Milius, Michael Cimino, Photography: Frank Stanley, Editor: Ferris Webster, Music: Lalo Schifrin, Art Director: Jack Collis

Cast: Clint Eastwood (Harry Callahan), Hal Holbrook (Lt. Briggs), Mitchell Ryan (Charlie McCoy), David Soul (Ben Davis), Tim Matheson (Phil Sweet), Robert Urich (John Grimes), Kip Niven (Red), Felton Perry (Early Smith), John Mitchum (DiGeorgio), Albert Popwell (Pimp), Adele Yoshioka (Sunny), Jack Kosslyn

Story: Harry's partner is killed in what appears to be a routine investigation. He gets a new, black partner, Early Smith. Investigating the killing, he discovers vigilantes are executing criminals. They turn out to be cops, led by Ben Davis, who defeated Harry in the police pistol shooting competition. Harry refuses to join the vigilantes' cause. His superior, Lt. Briggs, refuses to believe cops are involved. Smith is killed by a mailbox bomb, and Harry discovers a similar device left for him. Briggs, who is the head of the vigilantes, fails to kill Harry. Harry disposes of the cops and kills Briggs with the bomb meant for him.

Transformation: Harry is transformed from renegade cop to fighter of renegade cops.

Background: In the first of many Eastwood films that can be seen as direct replies to critical opprobrium, *Magnum Force* answers those who thought *Dirty Harry* was a fascist film by showing us what a really fascist police force would be like. "You didn't like Harry's violence? Well, this time we'll let Milius write the WHOLE movie!" "You think Harry is racist? Well, now he's got a black partner."

One scene is symbolic. When Harry is engaged in a shooting contest against the very Aryan über-cop Davis, he guns down a 'friendly' policeman target, and is told "You shot the good guy, Harry." As we all know, the good guy is Harry, iconic American lone wolf, and not necessarily the police. But Davis is, by implication, the man with the better, if not bigger, magnum (an image which would recur when co-writer Cimino wrote and directed *Thunderbolt And Lightfoot*).

Davis and his crew later try to recruit Harry to their side. Lined up on their motorcycles in black leather and mirror sunglasses, the three cops are like John Milius' idea of the ultimate irresistible macho fantasy. Sounding like film critics, they tell Harry, "All our heroes are dead…You, of all people, should understand that." Harry replies: "I'm afraid you've misjudged me."

Verdict: If Milius or Eastwood had directed this, it would be a small classic. As it is, Ted Post does not know how to handle the tensions and fetishistic imagery. 3/5

Impressed by Michael Cimino's part in the scriptwriting of *Magnum Force*, Clint bought his next screenplay, even though it came with the proviso that Cimino be allowed to make his debut as a director. The result was one of Eastwood's finest…

Thunderbolt And Lightfoot (1974)

Crew: Director: Michael Cimino, Producer: Robert Daley (Malpaso/United Artists), Screenplay: Michael Cimino, Photography: Frank Stanley, Editor: Ferris Webster, Music: Dee Barton, Art Director: Tambi Larsen

Cast: Clint Eastwood (John Doherty, Thunderbolt), Jeff Bridges (Lightfoot), George Kennedy (Red Leary), Geoffrey Lewis (Goody), Catharine Bach (Melody), June Fairchild (Gloria), Jack Dodson (Vault Manager), Bill McKinney (Crazy Driver), Burton Gilliam (Welder), Gary Busey (Curly), Dub Taylor (Gas Station Attendant), Claudia Lennear (Secretary)

Story: Disguised as a country preacher, bank robber John 'Thunderbolt' Doherty is hiding out from his ex-partners, Red and Goody, who believe he (and his now-dead former partner) double-crossed them by stealing the loot from a robbery. When they interrupt his sermon with shots, he escapes with the help of Lightfoot, who is passing by in a stolen car. As a friendship develops, they head for Montana, where the loot from the robbery of the Armoury is hidden in a schoolhouse, only to discover a brand new school built on the site. Red and Goody catch them but Doherty persuades them he didn't steal the loot. Lightfoot suggests they rob the Montana Armoury again. They take day jobs while preparing – Goody is an ice cream salesman. Tension builds between wise-guy Lightfoot and repressed Red. The robbery plan has Lightfoot dress as a woman to distract the night man in the alarm centre; after the theft they will hide in a drive-in, with Red & Goody in the trunk of the car. Entering the drive-in, a sneeze and a shirt-tail dangling from the trunk alert the staff, who call the police. In the ensuing chase, Goody is killed. Red pulls a gun, takes all the money and gives Lightfoot a brutal beating. Escaping, Red is chased down by police and killed by guard dogs in the department store where he was working. Thunderbolt and Lightfoot accidentally discover the schoolhouse, moved out of town as a museum, and recover the loot from the original job. As they head off into the sunset in the new Cadillac Lightfoot has always desired, Lightfoot dies as the result of the beating.

Transformation: Doherty moves from priest to robber, from worker to thief and from single man to partner to single again.

Background: Lacking the indulgence of *Heaven's Gate*, Cimino has never done anything better. *Thunderbolt And Lightfoot* is probably the definitive buddy movie, examining the romantic nature of the relationship with far more wit and visual flair than any of the subsequent self-conscious deconstructions. It also has classic road movie touches, including wonderfully insane monologues from McKinney and Taylor.

It's not just a simple matter of Jeff Bridges' Lightfoot taunting Red with his sexuality, dressing as a woman, or being Clint's date for the drive-in. The relationship between Red Leary and Goody is also complex. Goody is Puritan-speak for a wife (goodwife), and the two are an archetypal old married couple. A bullying husband and whining wife. Leary, as befits his name, both leers at the more dynamic relationship of the other pair, and is leery of it to the point of jealous rage.

The relationship of our eponymous couple is delineated clearly. When they pick up women, Thunderbolt would obviously rather be with Lightfoot. The robbery is merely a means to get to the drive-in, and in the school house scene they are a more comfortable tourist couple than the one they interrupt. Robin Wood famously analysed the cross-cutting in the robbery sequence as a form of love-making, which climaxes as Bridges, in drag, removes a pistol from the rear of his panties while Eastwood, having got his 20mm armour-piercing cannon erect, lets it explode into the vault. (This obviously influenced a similar cannon/vault penetration which figures heavily in the gay subtext of the recent British 'thriller' *Sexy Beast*.) When Lightfoot casts away drag, he dons Goody's clothes, becoming T'bolt's 'goody'. And the inevitable phallic cigars with which they celebrate their success turn into the film's final subtextual image, as Lightfoot's death causes Thunderbolt to break his own cigar.

Verdict: 5/5

Magnum Force made more money than *Thunderbolt And Lightfoot*, which Clint felt the studio hadn't promoted properly. For his first film since *Breezy*, Eastwood turned again to what looked like a sure thing: a best-selling novel that was a cross between James Bond and *Where Eagles Dare*.

The Eiger Sanction (1975)

Crew: Director: Clint Eastwood, Executive Producers: Richard D Zanuck/David Brown, Producer: Robert Daley (Universal/Malpaso), Screenplay: Warren B Murphy, Hal Dresner, Rod Whitaker, Novel: Trevanian, Photography: Frank Stanley, Editor: Ferris Webster, Music: John Williams, Art Directors: George Webb, Aurelio Cragnola, Climbing Advisor: Mike Hoover, Mountain Photography: John Cleare, Jeff Schoolfield, Peter Pilafian, Pete White

Cast: Clint Eastwood (Jonathan Hemlock), George Kennedy (Ben Bowman), Vonetta McGee (Jemima Brown), Thayer David (Dragon), Elaine Shaw (Miss Cereberus), Gregory Wolcott (Pope), Brenda Venus (George), Jack Cassidy (McHough)

Story: Professor Hemlock is a retired CIA assassin and mountain climber. Guess what? CIA director Dragon blackmails him out of retirement in return for the IRS ignoring his secret art collection. He assassinates (sanctions) two men who've killed a CIA agent but another agent, Jemima Brown, disguised as a stewardess, beds him and steals the IRS pardon back. Hemlock learns the two men he killed murdered a friend, and that another agent, Miles, betrayed them. He agrees to another sanction, which involves joining a team climbing the Eiger. One of the climbers is a traitor who Hemlock must unmask and kill. Training for the climb with Ben Bowman, he foils Miles' attempt to kill him, killing Miles and his bodyguard. In Switzerland, the climbing team is beset with jealous tension. The cuckolded climber dies in a sudden freeze, and the other two also die. Hemlock is saved by Ben, the traitor, who was forced into it because his daughter is an addict. Hemlock lets Ben go and convinces Dragon one of the dead men was the traitor.

Transformation: Professor to assassin. A rebirth à la *Unforgiven*.

Background: The downbeat nature of what should be an upbeat film is generally attributed to Eastwood's reaction to the death of one of the mountain-climbing stuntmen. Yet the transition from Dirty Harry to James Bond was never going to be easy. It's interesting to see Eastwood reprise elements of the Hemlock character in, say, *Absolute Power*, as if to say there was something in him after all.

The film isn't helped by the fact that in most versions the love scene with Vonetta McGee is severely edited. Reportedly, the actors continued long after the cameras ran out of film, before anyone dared interrupt. McGee's character can be seen as a climax, of sorts, to the black women, like Hallie in *The Beguiled* or the secretary in *Thunderbolt And Lightfoot*, with whom the Eastwood character had previously flirted unsuccessfully.

Although Trevanian (Rod Whitaker, himself a professor) did a draft of the script, the shooting script was done by Warren Murphy, a pulp novelist who was writing the Mack Bolan, Executioner novels. The idea that Clint, who gave Murphy his first film assignment, was reading those would fit into his very Reaganite political profile of the early 1980s.

Verdict: 2/5

This film marked the end of Malpaso's association with Universal. Frank Wells, who had been Eastwood's lawyer, was now at Warner Brothers, so Malpaso signed a deal with them. At the time, Clint's directing career appeared to be stagnating. Pictures directed by others had made more money and given him his best roles. But when Robert Daley encountered a novel by Forrest Carter, published in a small-press edition of 75, the result was Eastwood's first classic.

The Outlaw Josey Wales (1976)

Crew: Director: Clint Eastwood, Producer: Robert Daley (Warner Brothers/Malpaso), Screenplay: Philip Kaufman, Sonia Chernus, Novel: *Gone To Texas* by Forrest Carter, Photography: Bruce Surtees, Editor: Ferris Webster, Music: Jerry Fielding, Production Design: Tambi Larsen, Stunts: Walter Scott, Assistant Editor: Joel Cox, Production Assistant: Fritz Manes

Cast: Clint Eastwood (Josey Wales), Chief Dan George (Lone Waite), Sondra Locke (Laura Lee), John Vernon (Fletcher), Bill McKinney (Terrill), Geraldine Kearns (Little Moonlight), Paula Trueman (Grandma Sarah), Sam Bottoms (Jamie), Will Sampson (Ten Bears), John Russell (Bloody Bill Anderson), John Quade (Comanchero leader), Sheb Wooley (Travis), Royal Dano (Ten Spot), John Mitchum (Al), William O'Connell (Slim), Kyle Eastwood (Josey's son)

Story: When Union-supporting Red Legs kill his family and burn his farm, Josey Wales becomes the bloodiest of Bloody Bill Anderson's guerrillas. At war's end, Fletcher negotiates with the authorities for a peaceful surrender, but Terrill, the Red Leg leader, massacres the men with only Wales and Jamie escaping. Wales vows revenge on Terrill and Fletcher. Although Jamie soon succumbs to his wounds, Wales escapes and heads west, picking up Lone Waite along the way. He saves Little Moonlight from rape and then rescues Grandma Sarah and her simple daughter Laura Lee from Comancheros, taking them to the ranch her son owns in Texas. Wales makes peace with Ten Bears, ensuring his 'family' will be able to live peacefully, but he is discovered by bounty hunters and decides to move on. Before he can, the Red Legs catch up with him. His family defeats them, with Wales killing Terrill. Fletcher and Wales agree the war is over, and Wales is dead.

Transformation: Wales goes from family man to renegade to family man. And to 'dead' man.

Background: This is Eastwood's first great movie and arguably his finest. It can be seen as a relocation of the Leone hero into an American landscape, and as a rewriting of the classic Westerns of John Ford and John Wayne, with Wales building his own little community in the west and coming to terms with his need for personal revenge. Richard Schickel's analysis of the film is the highlight of his Eastwood biography. He also notes that the film is a meditation on the celebrity of the gunfighter; in Leone Westerns his heroes remain anonymous, in the American west, killers become celebrities. The film ends with Wales, the celebrity killer, denying his own existence.

The novel *Gone To Texas* was published in a vanity press edition of 75 copies, and reissued as *The Rebel Outlaw Josey Wales* by a small press in an edition which was not much bigger. Forrest Carter was supposedly a self-taught Cherokee poet. Carter was a wild drunken crazy man, but the rights to the book were snapped up cheaply. Given that Forrest Carter turned out to be Asa Carter, a former speech-writer for George Wallace, Ku Klux Klan organiser and vicious racist and anti-Semite, the film's message of eco-sympathy with the Indians seems particularly incongruous.

Sonia Chernus, by now Malpaso's story editor, did the treatment, but Philip Kaufman, fresh from writing and directing *The Great Northfield Minnesota Raid*, was hired to direct and rewrote the screenplay. His directing style soon clashed with Eastwood's. When Clint shot a scene himself while Kaufman was still searching for a location, Kaufman's firing was inevitable.

Kaufman cast Chief Dan George, who had played a similar role in *Little Big Man*, as Lone Waite, and his relaxed presence forms another perfect counterpoint to Clint's tightly-wrapped intensity.

Verdict: Orson Welles said *The Outlaw Josey Wales*, "belongs with the great Westerns…of Ford and Hawks and people like that." He was right. 5/5

Third Cycle: Locke, Stock Company & Two Joking Orang-Utans

The success of *The Outlaw Josey Wales* inaugurated a new cycle of Eastwood films. This cycle is defined first by the presence of Sondra Locke as Clint's leading lady and Malpaso in-house co-star. The team of Eastwood and Locke did not make people forget Tracy and Hepburn. If the first two cycles were an apprenticeship of sorts as actor and director, this cycle was Clint's apprenticeship as a producer. He used house directors to continue the Dirty Harry cycle and make the extremely profitable Clyde movies, while he made the Harry-ish *Gauntlet* and brought back Don Siegel for one last picture together. He also began to experiment with the offbeat: "Those smaller, different projects are probably what led cumulatively to films like *Unforgiven* and *In The Line Of Fire*…they taught me not to be afraid to step out and do something different."

The Enforcer (1976)

Crew: Director: James Fargo, Producer: Robert Daley (Warner Brothers/ Malpaso), Screenplay: Sterling Silliphant, Dean Reisner, Story: Gail Hickman, SW Shurr, Photography: Charles Short, Editors: Ferris Webster, Joel Cox, Music: Jerry Fielding, Art Director: Allen Smith, Stunts: Buddy Van Horn

Cast: Clint Eastwood (Harry Callahan), Tyne Daly (Kate Moore), Harry Guardino (Lt. Bressler), Bradford Dillman (Captain MacKay), John Mitchum (DiGeorgio), DeVeren Brookwalter (Bobby Maxwell), John Crawford (Mayor), Albert Popwell (Big Ed Mustapha), Adele Proom (Irene), Jocelyn Jones (Miki), Samantha Doane (Wanda), MG Kelly (Priest), Robert Hoy (Buchinski), Ronald Manning (Tex), Art Rimdzius (Porn Director), Fritz Manes

Story: The People's Revolutionary Strike Force kill Harry's partner during a raid on an arms store. Harry, who had been reassigned to personnel, is put back on the investigation but given a female partner with no street experience. Harry tracks down the terrorists, who are led by Bobby Maxwell, a former pimp looking to make money under revolutionary pretences. They kidnap the mayor, and hold him for ransom on Alcatraz. Kate is killed saving Harry's life. Harry frees the mayor and uses a rocket launcher to kill Bobby.

Transformation: Harry moves from chauvinist to women's libber.

Background: The thought behind *The Enforcer* is pretty simple: Harry extends his equal opportunity/equal abuse policy to women. Screenwriter

Silliphant's idea, as pitched to Clint, was "the absolute horror – it's truly Conradian – of Dirty Harry being saddled with a woman as a partner."

Silliphant wrote Don Siegel's *The Lineup*, a taut San Francisco-set crime drama, and won an Oscar for the screenplay for *In The Heat Of The Night*, but by the mid-1970s was turning out disaster blockbusters. Eastwood called him out of the blue, and when they met for lunch Silliphant pitched his idea. Eastwood decided Silliphant's script needed more narrative drive. He had another, called *Moving Target*, which involved Harry with a terrorist group. It had been written by two fans from Oakland and left at his Hog's Breath Inn in Carmel, where Clint eventually read it and commissioned a rewrite. Dean Reisner folded the two scripts together and shared the screenplay credit with Silliphant. Gail Hickman and SW Shurr got credit for the original story.

It opens with a killing scene that is cut closer to Leone than virtually anything else in Clint's career, but director Jim Fargo then settles down and delivers, in Ted Post fashion, Harry's usual battles against criminals, liberals and bureaucratic assholes, that last played with great gusto by Bradford Dillman. When Harry finds out he is being reassigned, he says "Personnel is for assholes." Dillman's slow burn as he reveals that he spent 10 years in personnel, triggers a classic scowl/grimace reaction from Eastwood.

Dirty Harry movies proved a springboard to success as a TV detective. *Magnum Force* propelled David Soul into *Starsky & Hutch* and Robert Urich hit it big in *Vega$* and *Spenser*. Tyne Daly, of course, reprised her role in *The Enforcer* in *Cagney & Lacey*.

Verdict: Watchable, with Dillman and Daly, but not much else. 2/5

The Gauntlet (1977)

Crew: Director: Clint Eastwood, Producer: Robert Daley (Warner Brothers/Malpaso), Screenplay: Michael Butler, Dennis Shryack, Photography: Rexford Metz, Editors: Ferris Webster, Joel Cox, Music: Jerry Fielding, Art Director: Allen Smith, Stunts: Buddy Van Horn

Cast: Clint Eastwood (Ben Shockley), Sondra Locke (Gus Mally), Pat Hingle (Josephson), William Prince (Blakelock), Michael Cavanaugh (Feyderspiel), Bill McKinney (Constable), Mara Corday (Matron), Carol Cook (Waitress), Samantha Doane, Art Rimdzius, Fritz Manes, Don Vadis, Roy Jenson

Story: Phoenix cop Shockley, an alcoholic loser, is ordered by Blakelock to extradite a prisoner, Gus Mally, from Las Vegas. Mally is convinced they will be killed before they get back, because she can testify against corrupt higher-ups in the Phoenix police. Shockley eventually realises that Mally is right and that he has been sent on the mission because he was expected to fail. They escape ambushes of ever-increasing firepower, until Shockley finally armour-plates a bus to confront Blakelock. Running a gauntlet of hundreds of cops who riddle the bus, they reach Blakelock and Mally shoots him dead.

Transformation: William Munny in reverse. Shockley gives up the drink and turns into Dirty Harry (with armour).

Background: Shockley is Drinking Harry, a more unfocused version of the bureaucrats' and criminals' worst nightmare. They use his weakness against him, showing what would happen if Harry were not, well, Harry. With this film Sondra Locke began her transformation from waif to whore. In the films that followed, Eastwood would subject her to on-screen abuse worthy of Brian DePalma's treatment of Nancy Allen.

The Gauntlet is an interesting failure. It is most interesting when the forces of paranoia are aligned against Shockley and Mally, and least interesting when Shockley finally becomes Dirty Harry, and pilots his armoured bus through the streets of Phoenix like Joe Kidd's train ploughing through Sinola. And yes, you'd think one of the hundreds of cops blasting away at them might have hit the bus' tires, if only by accident.

Verdict: 2/5

Every Which Way But Loose (1978)

Crew: Director: James Fargo, Producer: Robert Daley (Warner Brothers/ Malpaso), Screenplay: Jeremy Jo Kronsberg, Photography: Rexford Metz, Editor: Ferris Webster, Music: Snuff Garrett, Art Director: Elaine Ceyder

Cast: Clint Eastwood (Philo Beddoe), Manis (Clyde), Sondra Locke (Lynn Halsey-Taylor), Ruth Gordon (Ma), Geoffrey Lewis (Orville Boggs), Beverly D'Angelo (Echo), Hank Worden (Trailer Court Manager), Bill McKinney (Dallas), Don Vadis, Roy Jenson (Bikers), Fritz Manes (Bartender), Jeremy Jo Kronsberg (Bruno), George Orrison

Story: Philo, a trucker who moonlights as a bare-knuckle boxer, lives with his manager Orville, his landlady Ma and Clyde, an orang-utan he won in a fight. Philo falls for singer Halsey-Taylor, who has a jealous boyfriend. When she disappears after he has lent her money, he assumes the boyfriend has kidnapped her and sets off in pursuit, chased by a motorcycle gang he has offended and two cops he has beaten in a bar fight. Picking up Echo along the way, Philo loves and loses Halsey-Taylor again, defeats the gang, the cops (and some punch-happy meatpackers) before finally learning Halsey-Taylor has taken him for a ride. A wiser Philo takes a dive in a fight against ageing fighter Tank Murdock and returns home with his friends (and ape).

Transformation: Philo goes from love-sick fighter chasing woman to sadder but wiser fighter who's willing to lose and is happy to have his own ape.

Background: Inspired, no doubt, by the success of Burt Reynolds' redneck comedies, this film was Eastwood's biggest moneymaker to date. It may have fulfilled the needs of the audience at that time (remember, say, *The Dukes Of Hazzard*?) but it also says something about Eastwood's appeal and understanding of the little guy.

The comedy in this film and its sequel is deliberately broad. It reminds me of director Frank Tashlin's work, but James Fargo lacks the touch and, to be honest, Clint lacks the quick reactions comedy needs. (He's more of a slow-burn kind of guy.) The result is something like a Russ Meyer film with violence replacing sex as the mainspring of the story.

Eastwood examined the complexities of his on-screen persona in his previous two films, in which he first comes to grips with a female partner, and then plays second fiddle to a savvy hooker. This time Sondra Locke plays a barely-human female while Clint has his masculinity shown up by an ape. It was as if he were saying, "you think Harry's a chauvinist ape? I'll show you what a big ape really is!"

In retrospect, the most interesting aspect of the film is the relationship of Philo and Halsey-Taylor. Halsey-Taylor's retreat, via the nebulous boyfriend, and eventual suckering of Philo is an eerie foreshadowing of the off-screen relationship between the two stars.

Verdict: When a movie is best viewed for its insights into the Locke/Eastwood affair how high can you rate it? 1/5

Escape From Alcatraz (1979)

Crew: Director: Don Siegel, Executive Producer: Robert Daley, Producer: Don Siegel (Paramount/Malpaso), Screenplay: Richard Tuggle, Book: J Campbell Bruce, Photography: Bruce Surtees, Editors: Ferris Webster, Joel Cox, Music: Jerry Fielding, Production Design: Allen Smith

Cast: Clint Eastwood (Frank Lee Morris), Patrick McGoohan (Warden), Roberts Blossom (Doc), Jack Thibeau (Clarence), Paul Benjamin (English), Fred Ward (Anglin), Larry Hankin (Charlie Butts), Frank Ronzio (Litmus), Bruce M Fischer (Wolf), Don Siegel (Doctor), Carl Lumbly, Danny Glover (Inmates)

Story: Morris is transferred to escape-proof Alcatraz. After beating up Wolf, who tried to 'punk' him, Frank spends time in solitary. He emerges and finds company in Litmus, Doc and English. When the Warden takes away Doc's painting privileges because he dislikes Doc's portrait of him, Doc severs his own fingers. Morris decides to escape, aided by the Anglin brothers, whom he knew in Atlanta, and Butts, his neighbour. In a group effort, they plot the escape, aided by Litmus, who has a fatal heart attack when the Warden crumbles one of the chrysanthemums he and Doc had nurtured. The suspicious Warden aims to switch Morris' cell, but Wolf's release from solitary causes Morris to move up the escape. Frank's cell mate chickens out at the last minute. The other three disappear into the darkness. After they are gone, the Warden discovers a chrysanthemum, left in memory of Doc, on Angel Island but announces the escapees must have drowned. Soon after, Alcatraz is closed.

Transformation: Morris is transformed to prisoner and back to free man but, more importantly, he emerges from solitary into partnership with other people.

Background: This is Siegel's last great film, and if *The Shootist* was his elegy for John Wayne, you can look at this one as an elegy for himself. Morris in prison is an allegory of a lone director at the mercy of an insane studio system, who keeps his integrity and finally escapes into the eternal darkness. If Morris escapes by learning cooperation, you could argue the Eastwood-Siegel partnership provided each of them with their escapes as well.

However you interpret it, there have rarely been any films which have depicted the psychopathia of power and the isolation of the lonely resister to that power, more visually than Siegel does in this one. Darkness is the metaphor: Morris enters darkness three times: first into solitary, next into the hidden passages that will lead to escape and finally, with the two brothers, into the total darkness of freedom. It is no longer threatening but liberating.

However, the dynamic between the two directors had changed and they would do no other movies together. Although Siegel was now a proven director of A-hits, after this film he found as much difficulty getting new projects as he had when he was a proven commodity as a director of B-features.

Verdict: There are a handful of great prison movies; Siegel made two of them. This one is even better than *Riot In Cell Block 11*. 5/5

Although it might be too easy to say that working with Siegel reminded Eastwood of the kind of films he might like to direct, I doubt if it's coincidence that his next film as director was his most low-key since *Breezy*. Though commentators generally assume that Eastwood began alternating moneymaking low-quality projects with smaller, personal ones, a close look at the pattern of the films suggests that Eastwood wanted to stretch himself, as an actor or director, rather than keep the Malpaso bottom line healthy.

Bronco Billy (1980)

Crew: Director: Clint Eastwood, Executive Producer: Robert Daley, Producer: Dennis Hackin (Warner Brothers/Second Street/Malpaso), Screenplay: Dennis Hackin, Photography: David Worth, Editors: Ferris Webster, Joel Cox, Music Supervisor: Snuff Garrett, Music Director: Stephen Dorff, Art Director: Eugene Lourie, Camera Operator: Jack Green

Cast: Clint Eastwood (Bronco Billy), Sondra Locke (Antoinette Lilly), Scatman Crothers (Doc Lynch), Sam Bottoms (Leonard James), Geoffrey Lewis (John Arlington), Bill McKinney (Lefty), Don Vadis (Chief Big Eagle), Sierra Pecheur (Running Water), Hank Worden (Mechanic), Woodrow Parfrey (Canterbury), Walter Barnes (Sheriff), Kyle and Allison Eastwood (Orphans)

Story: Bronco Billy McCoy's Wild West show is falling on hard times. He meets Antoinette Lilly and recruits her to fill the (recurring) opening for an assistant (target) in his trick-shooting and knife-throwing act. Lilly is actually an heiress on the run from a marriage of convenience (for purposes of her father's will) to John Arlington. Arlington is arrested for her murder and her stepmother and lawyer pay him to plead guilty so that they can claim the inheritance.

When a fire burns Billy's big top, he abandons his principles and attempts to rob a train. At Dr Canterbury's asylum, where the patients are putting together a new big top sewn from American flags, Antoinette spots Arlington and she returns to New York to claim her fortune. Billy begins drinking, but Running Water summons her back for the first show under the new tent.

Transformation: Basically, Bronco Billy goes from ersatz hero to Real American Hero

Background: If Frank Capra were going to make a Clint Eastwood movie this would be it. Unlike Capra films, which often end with a ringing endorsement of the system we've just seen beaten by a single man, *Bronco Billy* makes no such contradictory assumption. If the dark side of Bronco Billy's dream had been more convincing and Sondra Locke had been a better actress then this would have been a classic. In both cases, script problems may share the blame. Antoinette is problematic throughout (we're hard pressed to see her attraction) and her progress from apparent heiress whore to dainty waif stretches credibility, as does the best-ignored sub-plot about her stepmother's efforts to have her declared dead.

Bronco Billy has the feel of something done too quickly. It is the kind of film which, for once, required a more leisurely approach than Clint brings to it. It looks slipshod at times. As Eastwood's career progressed, he was generally content to take a script he liked and film it, tinkering with it himself as he felt necessary. The days of calling in Dean Reisner or physically cutting and pasting with Don Siegel were long gone. There is something better lurking underneath the big top here. There's still a lot to like about it, but I look at it more as a dry run for *White Hunter, Black Heart* than the finished masterpiece it should be.

Verdict: Even with the reservations. 4/5

Any Which Way You Can (1980)

Crew: Director: Buddy Van Horn, Executive Producer: Robert Daley, Producer: Fritz Manes (Warner Brothers/Malpaso), Screenplay: Stanford Sherman, Photography: David Worth, Editors: Ferris Webster, Ron Spang, Music: Snuff Garrett/Stephen Dorff, Production Design: William J Creber

Cast: Clint Eastwood (Philo), Sondra Locke (Halsey-Taylor), Geoffrey Lewis (Orville), Ruth Gordon (Ma), William Smith (Jack Wilson), Harry Guardino (James Beekman), Michael Cavanaugh (Patrick Scarfe), Bill McKinney (Dallas), Don Vadis, Roy Jenson, John Quade

Story: Philo wants to retire from bare-knuckle boxing but the mob wants him to take one last fight, against old rival Wilson. They kidnap Halsey-Taylor to provide them with the leverage to make sure the fight happens. It does. Clyde the orang-utan, meanwhile, gets all the fun.

Transformation: The most interesting occurs off screen. Sondra Locke's character returns as Philo's girlfriend with no explanation for the changes in circumstances and in her nature.

Background: A movie which starts out as Clint's version of *The Quiet Man* (retired boxer forced into one last grand fight through the streets of a picturesque town – in this case Jackson Hole, Wyoming) turns into Buddy Van Horn's version of *Bringing Up Baby*, with Sondra Locke in the role of screwball comedy dame and the anonymous ape playing Clyde (Manis had retired) as Baby.

Verdict: Norman Mailer said he admired the Clyde movies. You can only admire them so far. 2/5

Firefox (1982)

Crew: Director: Clint Eastwood, Executive Producer: Fritz Manes, Producer: Clint Eastwood (Warner Brothers/Malpaso), Screenplay: Alex Lasker, Wendell Wellman, Novel: Craig Thomas, Photography: Bruce Surtees, Editors: Ferris Webster, Ron Spang, Music: Maurice Jarre, Art Directors: John Graysmark, Elayne Ceder, Special Visual Effects: John Dykstra

Cast: Clint Eastwood (Mitchell Gant), Freddie Jones (Kenneth Aubrey), David Huffman (Buckholz), Nigel Hawthorne (Piotr), Dimitra Arliss (Natalia), Warren Clarke (Pavel)

Story: Pilot Mitch Gant, Russian-speaking former Vietnam POW, is lured out of retirement and sent to the Soviet Union to steal a stealth fighter (Firefox) whose weapons systems are thought-controlled. After training in Britain, he is smuggled to Russia disguised as Leon Sprague. When the real Sprague is beaten to death, he assumes another identity and is smuggled across Russia by Pavel in a series of close calls which cause the return of his POW trauma. Finally reaching the Firefox base, he is helped by the plane's designers, Jewish dissidents, to overpower pilot Voskov and steal the plane. He escapes, defeating Voskov in a Firefox dogfight.

Transformation: Mitch is the man of a thousand (identical) faces, but they are all shadow games until he is reborn as an ace pilot.

Background: *Firefox* is Eastwood's *Kelly's Heroes,* a mishmash of styles and themes that clang resoundingly off each other. Always keenly aware of the trends, Eastwood here tacks a lot of Vietnam angst (*Deer Hunter*) onto a character who suffers flashbacks but apparently no real guilt. It all seems designed primarily to recreate a *Star Wars*-style dogfight. The real subtext here is Clint's role as the man of a thousand faces. When you have a face which is instantly recognisable this is a conceit which amounts to a knowing wink at the audience.

Verdict: As with *The Eiger Sanction*, Clint's style doesn't crank up suspense. 1/5

Honkytonk Man (1982)

Crew: Director: Clint Eastwood, Executive Producer: Fritz Manes, Producer: Clint Eastwood (Warner Brothers/Malpaso), Screenplay/Novel: Clancy Carlisle, Photography: Bruce Surtees, Editors: Ferris Webster, Joel Cox, Michael Kelly, Music: Snuff Garrett/Stephen Dorff, Production Design: Edward Carfagno

Cast: Clint Eastwood (Red Stovall), Kyle Eastwood (Whit), John McIntire (Grandpa), Verna Bloom (Emmy), Matt Clark (Virgil), Barry Corbin (Derwood), John Russell (Jack Wade), Charles Cyphers (Stubbs), Johnny Gimble (Bob Willis)

Story: Tubercular and drunken country singer Red Stovall returns to his sister's poor farm in the dust bowl. Trying to get the money to get to an audition at the Grand Ol' Opry, Red enlists the help of his nephew Whit to steal chickens but is caught. Whit gets Red out of jail and, over the objections of his father, accompanies Red to Nashville, joined by his grandfather, who wants to return to his roots. In Tulsa, Red is conned into taking part in a hold-up by Derwood, a promoter who owes him money. Red gets his money from Derwood's poker game, and Marlene, Derwood's aide who dreams of Nashville stardom, stows away in Red's car. When his father leaves, Red gets drunk and sleeps with Marlene. Red skips out, leaving Whit to get rid of Marlene. Red and Whit reach Nashville, where his audition, singing a song Whit has written, goes well until he has a coughing fit. Rather than go to a sanatorium, Red accepts an offer from a record company, finishing the record just before he dies. Whit and Marlene leave together. Red's song becomes a hit.

Transformation: The film attempts to let Red be reborn as a decent father figure, but really only death effects his transformation into a successful singer.

Background: An anti-hero in the action genre garners sympathy or identification from the audience because he can be placed easily into a situation which shows him in a positive light. In his comic movies, Eastwood makes the anti-hero less an inept hero than a dark one. Red's music and his world-weary stories are what make him appealing, yet these do not help him save himself. In the poignant social context of the depression family, *Honkytonk Man* seems to undercut its own aims by allowing Red no real salvation other than stardom.

It's really about Red's inability to become, even symbolically, a family man. That inability is set against the reluctance of Virgil to let his son leave the dead-end life of the farm, and to some extent against Grandpa's failure to 'go the distance' with his son. In the end, Red's dissolute life is justified by his musical success. Eastwood told Tim Cahill that Red was based on some self-destructive people he knew. "He's been a coward in his time," he said. "He won't face up to his ambitions."

Verdict: 3/5

Sudden Impact (1983)

Crew: Director: Clint Eastwood, Executive Producer: Fritz Manes, Producer: Clint Eastwood (Warner Brothers/Malpaso), Screenplay: Joseph C Stinson, Story: Earl Smith, Charles Pierce, Photography: Bruce Surtees, Editor: Joel Cox, Music: Lalo Schifrin, Production Design: Edward Carfagno, Stunts: Buddy Van Horn

Cast: Clint Eastwood (Harry Callahan), Sondra Locke (Jennifer Spencer), Pat Hingle (Chief Jannings), Albert Popwell (Horace King), Bradford Dillman (Captain Briggs), Paul Drake (Mickey), Mara Corday (Waitress), James McEachin (Barnes), Audrie Neenan (Ray)

Story: Harry, in hot water as usual over his methods, is sent out of town to investigate a murder where the victim was shot in the genitals and head. Breaking up a hold-up, he tells the hostage taker to "make his day." He immediately antagonises local Chief Jennings. He meets artist Jennifer Spencer, who is the murderer, and she kills a second time. Spencer is getting revenge for a gang rape and, when the third victim dies, Harry makes a connection to a photo on the Chief's office wall. Questioning Ray, a lesbian who set up the rape, Harry arrests Mickey, one of the rapists, as Jennifer lurks outside. Mickey is bailed and comes after Harry with two thugs, but only kills Harry's ex-partner. Jannings interrupts Jennifer about to kill victim five, his son, and admits having let the rape go because his son was involved. Mickey shoots Jannings with Jennifer's gun and tries to rape her again but he is impotent. Jennifer escapes to a fairground, where Harry kills Mickey. He lets Jennifer go and pins her five killings on the dead man.

Transformation: Harry is transformed from law and order absolutist into a believer in situational ethics.

Background: It was perhaps not so ironic that Ronald Reagan should make such use of the phrase 'go ahead, make my day" when it came from Harry's least successful case, the one where he decides to let a killer walk. Jennifer's admiration for Harry as one of an "endangered species" recalls that of the leather cops from *Magnum Force* but, though feminist vengeance may have been a relatively politically correct way of showing Harry's sympathetic side, the deviance of the gang of rapists (one is a bull dyke, another reads porno) makes Harry seem more like Oprah Winfrey with a gun. It's more significant that, almost a decade ahead of *Thelma & Louise*, Eastwood was directing a film in which Dirty Harry could accept a woman's vigilante response to rape, and the critics didn't cry that he'd accepted fascism.

Verdict: With a more convincing actress than Locke this would rate a mark higher. 2/5

Tightrope (1984)

Crew: Director: Richard Tuggle, Producer: Clint Eastwood (Warner Brothers/Malpaso), Screenplay: Tuggle, Photography: Bruce Surtees (who became ill during the filming, and Jack Green took over), Editor: Joel Cox, Music: Lennie Niehaus, Production Design: Edward Carfagno, Stunts: Buddy Van Horn

Cast: Clint Eastwood (Wes Block), Geneviève Bujold (Beryl Thibodeaux), Dan Hedeya (Molonari), Alison Eastwood (Amanda), Jennifer Beck (Penny), Marco St John (Rolf), Rebecca Pearl (Becky), Regina Richardson (Sarita), Randi Brooks (Jamie), Margaret Howell (Judy Harper), Rebecca Clemons, David Valdes, Fritz Manes

Story: A serial killer is preying on prostitutes in New Orleans' French Quarter, and Detective Wes Block shares the killer's penchant for handcuffs and hookers (his wife has recently left him and their two daughters). Block knows, in both senses, some of the victims and becomes involved with Becky, who worked with another of them. As bodies continue to fall, Block becomes attracted to Beryl, who runs a rape crisis centre and is raising a stink because the murders have not been solved. The killer sends Block off on a wild goose chase, eventually killing Becky and leaving behind Block's tie – the tie he took from another prostitute he killed after Block visited her. Plagued with nightmares in which he sees himself as the killer, Block is convinced by Beryl that he can indeed manage a normal relationship. He traces the killer to the Dixie Brewery, where he turns out to be an ex-cop rapist Block arrested years before. The killer attacks Block's kids, is driven off and strikes at Beryl. Block saves her and chases the killer to his death beneath a train.

Transformation: One of Eastwood's key rebirths. By relinquishing control to Beryl, Wes overcomes his "Block", and becomes a functioning lover, father and detective.

Background: Or 'Filthy Harry.' One of the many explanations for Harry's nickname was that he appeared to enjoy 'dirty' pastimes like peeping. In *Tightrope* we are presented with a Harry who is far dirtier, in what was the strongest examination of the character to date. The script pulls some punches. Harry may be a pervert but he's also a devoted single parent. He's a habitué of hookers but he also gets the ultimate feminist to fall for him.

Said feminist may be the boss of a rape crisis centre, but she'll need to be rescued by a man.

This is a self-consciously dark movie, and all the better for that, but one wonders if Richard Tuggle's failure to reappear in the Eastwood universe may reflect some problems with the overall concept – the film ends up chasing the villain through a freightyard rather than chasing Wes' demons down his own dark alleys. In his *Guardian* interview, Eastwood was noticeably silent when asked about Tuggle's role in this film and his subsequent career. Yet, when David Thomson said he preferred the characters who show "doubt and vulnerability," Eastwood said, "I have such feelings myself, or I would never have attacked something like *Tightrope*." Certainly he enjoyed the idea that Wes might himself be the killer, even looping the killer's voice with his own early in the film.

The real strength of *Tightrope* is Geneviève Bujold, the finest female lead in any Eastwood film. Her inner presence is the female version of his and Bujold, while lacking the stature, is able to project the intensity needed without sacrificing her appeal.

Verdict: With a firmer hand at the helm, to get more out of Clint, this would have been a classic. 4/5

City Heat (1984)

Crew: Director: Richard Benjamin, Producer: Fritz Manes (Warner Brothers/Malpaso/Deliverance), Screenplay: Sam O Brown (Blake Edwards), Joseph C Stinson, Photography: Nick McLean, Editor: Jacqueline Cambas, Music: Lennie Niehaus, Production Design: Edward Carfagno, Stunts: Buddy Van Horn

Cast: Clint Eastwood (Lt. Speer), Burt Reynolds (Mike Murphy), Jane Alexander (Addy), Madeline Kahn (Caroline), Rip Torn (Primo Pitt), Irene Cara (Ginny Lee), Richard Roundtree (Dehl Swift), Tony LoBianco (Leon Coll), Robert Davi (Nino), William Sanderson (Lonnie Ash), John Hancock (Fat Freddie), Hamilton Camp, George Orrison

Story: Down-at-heel private eye Murphy is helped fighting off repo men by his former police colleague Speer, who's sweet on Murphy's secretary Addy. Murphy's partner Swift is playing two gangsters (Pitt and Coll) against each other, using ledgers stolen from Coll. Pitt suspects a double-cross and kills Swift, but Speer saves Swift's girlfriend Ginny. Coll picks up Murphy, who offers to return the ledgers for the $50,000 Swift had been promised. Pitt kidnaps Murphy's girlfriend Caroline and kills Ginny, but Murphy finds the ledgers. Bringing them to Addy, he gets caught in a cross-fire between Pitt's and Coll's men. Speer arrives to stop that. Murphy confronts Pitt, claiming he's booby-trapped the ledgers with dynamite. Murphy and Speer shoot it out with Pitt and kill him. They rescue Caroline, but Coll kidnaps Addy. Murphy hands the ledgers over to him, and Coll is blown up by the dynamite.

Background: A doomed project which must have seemed like a can't miss blockbuster teaming middle America's two favourite stars in a light-hearted action film. Originally conceived by Blake Edwards and called *Kansas City Jazz*, the idea was sold to Clint while Edwards and Reynolds collaborated on their remake of Truffaut's *The Man Who Loved Women*. Edwards actually gave the script to Sondra Locke, promising her the Caroline role (apparently the original intent was also for Julie Andrews to play Addy). Eastwood was never happy with Edwards' more extravagant style. Edwards was eventually squeezed out and Warner Brothers took over the whole film. Clint brought Stinson in for a final rewrite of the script. Having won the battle for control, many of the Malpaso stock company were signed, and Richard Benjamin was finally hired to direct. Benjamin, whose first film, *My Favourite Year*, had shown a nice comic touch, had no experience with action films.

With Edwards gone, so was Andrews. Clint gave Madeline Kahn the Locke role and added some spark. Jane Alexander took Andrews' role, joining Verna Bloom and Carrie Snodgress in Clint's panoply of strong females in smaller roles. Burt Reynolds broke his jaw during the filming, which led to an addiction to painkillers. Even so, his work with Clint is sometimes amusing, as is the over-the-top playing by LoBianco and Torn.

The problem is the film is not focussed. Richard Roundtree is the one who makes the whole plot go but we know very little about him. The mix between action and comedy is not handled nearly as well as, say, the fight scene of *My Favourite Year* because nobody really knows whether the film is action or comedy. The result is the empty star vehicle it may have been conceived as, but certainly didn't have to be.

Verdict: 2/5

Pale Rider (1985)

Crew: Director: Clint Eastwood, Executive Producer: Fritz Manes, Producer: Clint Eastwood (Warner Brothers/Malpaso), Screenplay: Michael Butler, Dennis Shryack, Photography: Bruce Surtees, Editor: Joel Cox, Music: Lennie Niehaus, Production Design: Edward Carfagno, Stunts: Buddy Van Horn, Associate Producer: David Valdes

Cast: Clint Eastwood (Preacher), Michael Moriarty (Hull Barrett), Carrie Snodgress (Sarah Wheeler), Richard Dysart (Coy LaHood), John Russell (Marshal Stockburn), Sydney Penny (Megan), Christopher Penn (Josh

LaHood), Richard Kiel (Club), Doug McGrath (Spider), John Dennis Johnson (Tucker), Billy Drago (Mather), Buddy Van Horn (Driver)

Story: Hydraulic mine tycoon LaHood gets his men to raid Carbon Canyon and terrorise the small miners. They attack Hull Barrett in town, but he is saved by a stranger they call Preacher. He returns with Hull, meets Hull's intended, single mother Sarah, and her daughter Megan, who sees Preacher as the answer to her prayers for help. Preacher, who has a pattern of bullet holes on his back, drives away further attacks. The miners find gold and turn down LaHood's offer to buy them out, knowing they will have to face Marshal Stockburn and his six deputies if they do. Preacher disappears but returns in time to save Megan from rape by LaHood's son. He and Hull destroy LaHood's hydraulic works. Preacher kills the deputies and then Stockburn, who has recognised him. Preacher rides off as Megan calls for him to come back.

Transformation: Preacher is reborn explicitly to enact his vengeance.

Background: This was Bruce Surtees' last Eastwood film and it is a beautiful one. It's hampered by an over-reliance on *Shane* (Sydney Penny's performance making Brandon DeWilde look hard-edged), especially at the end. "We love you, Preacher" has none of the power of "Shane, come back."

Preacher as eco-Shane is a twist (at the time strip-mining was a contentious issue, revolving around Reagan's bonehead Secretary of the Interior, James Watt) but sets up a counterpoint to Preacher's mysticism, which is occasionally far-fetched. Snodgress is perfect as the woman wondering if she should live with a man who may be a shell of a real man, and Moriarty does well conveying that character. John Russell – one of those TV cowboys who didn't escape from the box like Clint did--also appeared in *The Outlaw Josey Wales* and *Honkeytonk Man*, but this is his best role.

Verdict: It's the weakest of the Westerns Eastwood has directed but I like the performances and the look. 3/5

Eastwood's career appeared to be stalled at this point and perhaps the lack of success of his more personal films, like *Bronco Billy*, had raised questions. At the same time, his personal life was also in turmoil, and he allowed himself to be distracted from film-making for long enough to become mayor of Carmel. Chicken or egg? It's hard to say, but Clint would emerge from this period with a clear vision of where he was going as a filmmaker.

Mid-Life Crisis I: Eastwood In Love

When the relationship between Eastwood and Sondra Locke became public, and his wife Maggie sued for divorce, it shattered Eastwood's public image as a blue-collar guy with an everyday marriage. In reality, from the start Clint viewed his marriage as open and indulged in various affairs, but until Locke he rarely, if ever, brought them home. Entire biographies have been devoted to painting a tabloid picture of Eastwood's love life. Patrick McGilligan even blames him, via innuendo, for Jean Seberg's suicide.

Although he has had affairs with many of his co-stars, and brief encounters with some big names (among them Jayne Mansfield and Catherine Deneuve), most of his longer-term relationships appear to have been low-key, with the women content to remain in the background. He has fathered at least eight children by five different women. An early child by an unnamed mother was apparently put up for adoption.

In addition to Kyle (born 1968) and Alison (born 1972), his children with Maggie, he fathered a daughter, Kimber (born 1964) with Roxanne Tunis, an extra and stunt woman on *Rawhide*. While his relationships with Locke and Frances Fisher were in flux he had two children, Scott (born 1986) and Kathryn (born 1988) with Jacelyn Reeves, a stewardess and Carmel neighbour. His relationship with Fisher produced Francesca (born 1993) in the same year he met local news reporter Dina Ruiz (shades of *The Dead Pool*). Clint and Dina married in 1996 and their daughter, Morgan, was born the same year. Clint was 66 years old.

Maggie's divorce became final in 1984. The settlement was $25-30 million, but the two were apparently on better terms apart than they had been together. In the immediate aftermath of the divorce, while his life was at its most chaotic, he directed an episode of Steven Spielberg's television series *Amazing Stories*, which gave a rare insight into his relationship with Locke.

Vanessa In The Garden (1985)

Crew: Director: Clint Eastwood, Executive Producer and Screenplay: Steven Spielberg, Producer: David Vigel, Photography: Robert Stevens, Editor: Jo Ann Fogle, Music: Lennie Niehaus, 30 mins, TV

Cast: Harvey Keitel (Byron), Sondra Locke (Vanessa), Beau Bridges (Teddy)

Background: In this fascinating story, Locke plays a ghost who returns to Keitel (if only, perhaps, in his imagination) to inspire him back to his impressionist painting. Van Gogh cut off his ear, Keitel merely burned the paintings with Locke in them. Eastwood's direction of a ghost story is as sure as his handling of horror in *Play Misty For Me*, but opts for slower, psychological effects rather than shock. His play with images from the canvas, from mirrors and through windows, all accomplished with camera moves, is perfect. The casting is less perfect. Keitel's artist hardly seems able to pine, Bridges' agent is too effete and Locke, ethereal enough as a ghost, is puzzling enough as Eastwood's muse, much less Byron's. It was the lowest rated episode of the series, indicating Eastwood's faded box-office allure.

Verdict: 3/5

The 1989 break-up with Locke was acrimonious in the extreme. By this time he was already involved with Frances Fisher. Locke's first palimony suit was settled out of court, with Locke getting a three-year $1.5 million development deal with Warner Brothers. She had already directed one film, *Ratboy* (1986), which was produced by Malpaso, with Manes, Carfagno, Cox and Niehaus all playing their Malpaso roles. It starred Locke and Robert Townsend, but created deeper problems with Eastwood because of the input of Locke's husband and former Svengali, Gordon Anderson. Her second feature, also produced by Warner Brothers, was *Impulse* (1990) starring Theresa Russell. Both films have an offbeat quality which reflects Locke's largest asset as an actress, an off-centre spacey wistfulness. Much as Locke would claim Eastwood had stifled her career, as an actress she is Veronica Lake without the emotional range, and starring roles outside Malpaso were always unlikely. In 1996 Locke sued Warner Brothers and Eastwood, alleging her development deal had been a sham, with its costs written off against *Unforgiven*. Just before a jury trial was about to conclude, Eastwood again settled. Locke directed one more film, *Do Me A Favor* (1996), with Roseanne Arquette and wrote her side of the story in *The Good, The Bad And The Very Ugly* (1997).

Also in 1996 Eastwood co-produced *The Stars Fell On Henrietta* on behalf of Frances Fisher, who starred along with Robert Duvall, Aidan Quinn and Brian Dennehy. Directed by James Keach from a script by Phil Railsback, Bruce Surtees and Joel Cox performed their usual Malpaso roles.

Again, whether cause or effect is unsure, but the disruption in Clint's private life coincided with his election as mayor of Carmel, California, in 1986. There was much speculation that Clint would give up film and start a second career in politics. After all, another actor had come from Californian politics to become President of the United States. But Clint's election, backed by a professional effort in a small community, led to two years as mayor in which he took local issues seriously, postponed much of his film work and basically managed to get through the zoning changes he wanted.

Eastwood's applications for his Hog's Breath Inn (inspired by pubs he visited with Richard Burton) and an office complex next door had been denied twice by Carmel's council. The town was torn between residents who discouraged commercialism (an infamous ordinance banned eating ice cream cones in the street) and businessmen hoping to increase tourism. Of course, having Clint as mayor hardly kept tourists away, so the council learned it would have been easier to be more understanding to Clint in the first place.

Long before all this, *Dirty Harry* had forced Clint into the political spotlight. He was regarded as the heir to John Wayne's reactionary politics. Eastwood publicly supported Nixon in 1972 and Reagan later on, but by 1992 would back Ross Perot. Although eminently conservative with both big and little Cs, Eastwood is also antagonistic to the right's moral crusades. If he weren't it would make him as much a hypocrite as Henry Hyde or Newton Gingrich. He has always been in the forefront of racial equality and his films have opened more and more to women's issues as well. His personal politics might best be described as libertarian.

This might include his 1982 foray into private armies. Eastwood, the reader of The Executioner novels, got involved with a self-proclaimed Mack Bolan, Colonel Bo Gritz and his schemes to 'rescue' American POW's allegedly held in Laos. Gritz gathered other celebrity backers, including William Shatner. Clint tried to get President Reagan's support and used Warner Brothers' jet to fly 'soldiers' in for manoeuvres at his ranch. The result in Laos was two of Gritz's men dead and the repatriation of some bones which Eastwood says were not even human. He has publicly distanced himself from such people ever since. Smart move.

Fourth Cycle: Personal & American Icons

When Clint refused to seek a second term as mayor in 1988, he began to put the crises of the 1980s behind him. His only film during his mayoralty revisited the American hero with whose western roles and political stances Eastwood was often compared.

Heartbreak Ridge (1986)

Crew: Director: Clint Eastwood, Executive Producer: Fritz Manes, Producer: Clint Eastwood (Warner Brothers/Malpaso), Screenplay: James Carabatsos, Photography: Jack N Green, Editor: Joel Cox, Music: Lennie Niehaus, Production Design: Edward Carfagno, Stunts: Buddy Van Horn

Cast: Clint Eastwood (Tom Highway), Marsha Mason (Aggie), Everett McGill (Major Powers), Moses Gunn (Sgt. Webster), Bo Svenson (Roy Jennings), Mario Van Peebles (Stitch Jones), Eileen Heckart (Little Mary), Tom Villard (Profile), Boyd Gaines (Lt. Ring), Arlen Dean Snyder (Choozoo), Peter Koch (Swede), Richard Venture (Colonel Myers), Rebecca Perle/Pearl (Girl In Shower)

Story: Gunnery Sgt. Highway is bailed out of the drunk tank and reassigned to an incompetent recon platoon in Major Powers' regiment. On the way to his new unit he is conned by rock musician Jones, who turns out to be part of his unit. Highway wins over his men and his bookish Lieutenant by standing up to Powers. He also discovers his ex-wife is waitressing at a nearby bar. His attempts to win her back include boning up on 'new man' vocabulary, but when she throws him out he winds up in the drunk tank. She bails him out, but later at a formal dance she tells him her boss has asked her to marry him. Before she can tell him her reply, the marines are ordered back to barracks for their invasion of Grenada. His men rescue American students then disobey orders and take a Cuban command post – they call in air support using Jones' credit card. Powers threatens to court-martial them but is overruled by combat veteran Myers. Aggie is waiting for Highway when he returns a hero.

Transformation: Highway transforms himself into a caring man, and transforms young and decadent Americans into conquerors of mighty Grenada. He also transforms the American soldier back to his victorious World War II image.

Background: This is less a war movie than Clint's exploration of the classic received image of John Wayne. For all that Wayne's star status was honed by Ford and Hawks as a cowboy, the John Wayne who took the blame for the Vietnam war was the one who played in combat films from lesser directors and, according to modern myth, never died. In *Heartbreak Ridge* Clint only pretends to die, while *Sands Of Iwo Jima*, of which this film is very much an examination, was one in which Wayne actually was killed.

Sadly, *Heartbreak Ridge* rings hollow, as hollow as the assertion that the 'win' in Grenada somehow evens the score for the 'tie' in Korea and 'loss' in Vietnam (Highway's platoon, and its Lieutenant, resemble the eponymous soliders of Oliver Stone's *Platoon*, but in Highway's Vietnam "we lost the war but won the battles"). Grenada is the victory of American credit cards over a Cuban army that appears to be no more than a Dirty Dozen with a couple of Russian tanks.

Eastwood the director seems unsure of the character played by Clint the actor. He gives Highway more approving reaction shots in this film than in any three of his serious films put together, as if he's playing to a gallery. Perhaps that's because Eastwood had major problems with the Pentagon. Originally, the Army turned down approval saying, according to McGilligan, that Highway was 'an outdated stereotype.' By switching the story to the Marines, they got approval but the result is a military mess. The recon platoon are already Marines but are apparently left alone to behave like a high-school gang. Highway fought in Korea in the Army and then became a Marine, making him far too old for what he's doing (though younger than Moses Gunn).

Verdict: The Army was right. 2/5

After that false start, and with Carmel politics behind him, Clint began this cycle of films in earnest. In the next seven years he directed six films, five of which are first rate and three of those are outstanding. This series began with *Bird*.

John Wayne was America's idol, but Charlie Parker was Clint's personal hero. Eastwood said his smaller, personal films of the early 1980s had prepared him for *Unforgiven*, but *Honkytonk Man* was certainly direct preparation for *Bird*. Bernard Tavernier's *'Round Midnight* encouraged him. After premiering *Pale Rider* in Cannes, Eastwood had dined with Tavernier, who as a critic had been supportive of him. Eastwood returned the favour by convincing Warner Brothers to finance *'Round Midnight* to the tune of $4 million, despite their reservations over the casting of saxophonist Dexter Gordon in the lead. *'Round Midnight* was a critical success and made some money. But Clint's film would turn out to be not so much about jazz as about the dark side of creative genius…

71

Bird (1988)

Crew: Director: Clint Eastwood, Executive Producer: David Valdes, Producer: Clint Eastwood (Warner Brothers/Malpaso), Screenplay: Joel Oliansky, Photography: Jack Green, Editor: Joel Cox, Music: Lennie Niehaus, Production Design: Edward Carfagno

Cast: Forest Whitaker (Charlie 'Bird' Parker), Diane Venora (Chan Richardson), Michael Zelnicker (Red Rodney), Samuel E Wright (Dizzy Gillespie), Keith David (Buster), Michael McGuire (Brewster), James Handy (Esteves), Damon Whitaker (Young Bird), Arlen Dean Snyder (Dr Heath), Sam Robards (Moscowitz), Hamilton Camp, Jo de Winter

Story: The story of Charlie Parker, the great alto sax player and bebop innovator, who died aged 35 due to drug and alcohol abuse, is told through a series of flashbacks, cued by a cymbal tossed at him by a drummer to get him off stage when he made his public debut aged 15. It traces his marriage to jazz groupie Chan Richardson, the tragedy of their daughter's death, his creative partnership with Dizzy Gillespie and his association with the white trumpeter Red Rodney.

Transformation: There is no rebirth in this film, apart from Parker's music. His tortured genius is pacified only through drugs and, in the end, they kill him

Background: Viewed 13 years on, *Bird* reveals depths which far outstrip the contemporary criticisms of it. Yes, the Red Rodney sub-plot, having made its points about Parker's white fans and the white disciples who followed him into be bop and drug addiction, goes on far too long (Parker once explained he made his music difficult so white bands couldn't copy it), but as a way of relating both the music and the character to a contemporary audience, it makes sense. The decision to redo the back-up music, while keeping Parker's solos, also seems far less serious a flaw than many jazz fans claimed at the time. The back-up music may be mellower than the original but Parker's own sound stands out more distinctly.

The film makes very little of racial tension and bigotry. Apart from Dizzy's fine speech about overcoming prejudiced stereotypes, the segregation issue is dealt with lightly as Red 'passes' as an albino black, a strange reversal of the bigotry musicians encountered in New York. Parker suffers at the hands of the New York police because of his drug abuse, not because of his race. This is typical of many Eastwood movies where people are, literally, colour-blind. No one in *Unforgiven* ever remarks on Ned's colour. Butch in *Perfect World* accepts the sharecropper as an equal. This is admirable in a general sense but dangerous in a specific one, when real tensions, dangers and agonies are ignored. Likewise, the references to the serious hostility with which bebop was greeted in many jazz circles is sloughed off into off-hand comments by musicians.

Race or jazz are not Eastwood's main concern in *Bird*. The adoring jazz-fan doctor in Bellevue could be Clint himself, because *Bird* is, above all else, about tortured genius, the difficulty such genius has in trying to live a 'normal' life and the pain a supportive woman faces when acting as both inspiration and anchor. As such, it would be best to compare it to films about painters like *Pollock* (also directed by an actor), rather than to other jazz films.

Verdict: Whitaker won a deserved best actor award at Cannes for this. 4/5

After *Bird*, Eastwood continued his involvement with jazz film. He bought the French and Italian rights to the documentary *The Last Of The Blue Devils*. Released in those countries as 'Clint Eastwood presents,' it paved the way for *Bird*. Its director, Bruce Ricker, would later make an excellent documentary about Clint. He also got Warner Brothers to give Ricker the finance for Charlotte Zwerin's documentary about Thelonius Monk, *Straight No Chaser*, on which Eastwood took executive producer credit. He took the same credit a decade later on *Monterey Jazz Festival*, an event he'd showcased in *Play Misty For Me*.

Eastwood is always accused of alternating the personal and the profitable, but I suspect that after the hard work on *Bird* he simply needed a directing break. A lighter Dirty Harry vehicle awaited.

The Dead Pool (1988)

Crew: Director: Buddy Van Horn, Producer: David Valdes (Warner Brothers/Malpaso), Screenplay: Steve Sharon, Story: Steve Sharon, Durk Pearson, Sandy Shaw, Photography: Jack Green, Editors: Joel Cox, Ron Spang, Music: Lalo Schifrin, Production Design: Edward Carfagno, Stunts: Richard Farnsworth

Cast: Clint Eastwood (Harry Callahan), Patricia Clarkson (Samantha Walker), Liam Neeson (Peter Swan), Evan C Kim (Al Quan), David Hunt (Harlan Rook), Michael Currie (Captain Donnelly), Michael Goodwin (Lt. Ackerman), Darwin Gillett (Patrick Snow), Anthony Charnota (Lou Janero), Christopher Beale (DA), Jim Carrey (Johnny Squares)

Story: The overdose death of rocker Squares on the set of Swan's horror film *Hotel Satan* leads to Harry being assigned to make nice with newswoman Walker. Walker is sent a list showing that Squares was part of a 'dead pool' where the players choose a list of celebrities and win if their pick dies first. Squares and Harry's names are both on Swan's list. As more victims drop, Harry believes Swan is being set up, and Swan recalls a manic fan, Rook. Harry and new partner Al trace Rook, but Rook kidnaps Walker. Harry loses his magnum to Rook but kills him with a harpoon.

Transformation: This one is so by the numbers, and Harry is reborn as a joking, media-friendly, team player. Sort of.

Background: Though this is the fifth, and thus far last, of the canonical Dirty Harry films (*Rookie* is a Harry film in all but name and motorcycles) it should be noted that at least two other Harry screenplays which Eastwood optioned were made with other actors: Fred Williamson's *The Big Score* and Chuck Norris' *Code Of Silence*.

Dead Pool is really Buddy Van Horn's *Big Sleep*. Harry moves among the celebrity world of film-makers and rock stars. There's a gangster sub-plot which sees the mob protecting Harry after he cons the mob boss in prison. One of the victims turns out to be a San Francisco film critic not a million miles away from Eastwood's old nemesis, Pauline Kael. She gets the most deserved critic's death since Diana Rigg and Vincent Price were at work in *Theatre Of Blood*.

The TV reporter, played by Clarkson, provides the coolest love interest in any Eastwood film. Although she pursues Harry and they spend the night together, we never see them kiss. Clarkson, who begins the film as a classic wannabe, trying to do a man's work, appears unwilling to reduce herself completely to waif status, though she does manage a few admiring glances when required.

Having gone through black, Latino, women and fat Italian partners, Harry's latest sidekick is an Oriental called Al. He is assigned for good PR value, can't keep up with the old man's jogging but does do a fine Jackie Chan imitation.

Verdict: Tongue in cheek and fun. You've got a magnum? Mine's a harpoon. 3/5

Pink Cadillac (1989)

Crew: Director: Buddy Van Horn, Executive Producer: Michael Gruskoff, Producer: David Valdes (Warner Brothers/Malpaso), Screenplay: John Eskow, Photography: Jack Green, Editor: Joel Cox, Music: Stephen Dorff, Production Design: Edward Carfagno

Cast: Clint Eastwood (Tommy Nowack), Bernadette Peters (Lou Ann McGuinn), Timothy Carhart (Roy), Michael Des Barres (Alex), John Dennis Johnson (Waycross), Geoffrey Lewis (Ricky Z), Bill McKinney (Bartender), Jimmie F Skaggs (Billy), Bill Mosley (Darrell), Michael Champion (Ken Lee), James Cromwell (Motel Owner), William Hickey (Burton), Paul

Benjamin (Judge), Frances Fisher (Dinah), Jim Carrey (Elvis Impersonator), Mara Corday (Stick Lady)

Story: When Lou Ann skips bail after taking the fall for her husband's counterfeiting scheme with his Aryan brotherhood prison buddies, Nowack is hired to bring her back. In her husband's beloved Caddy is a huge cache of counterfeit bills, which she discovers. Nowack catches her and, although she starts off scamming him, he eventually becomes sympathetic. They team up to rescue her child, who was kidnapped by the gang, and get away together.

Transformation: Confirmed bachelor Nowack is transformed into family man, and gets a pink car in the process

Background: The last of Clint's trilogy of 'Buddy' movies starts off as if Philo Beddoe has been recruited to play Dirty Harry, but becomes Van Horn's version of *His Girl Friday*. Like Van Horn's other two Eastwood vehicles, this is surprisingly pleasant but goes nowhere – a sort of a pink Cadillac on blocks. Here the major problem is the lack of on-screen chemistry between Peters and Clint. The actress appears to be bouncing off him literally as she wavers between waif and worthy.

Clint also gets to play a man of a thousand faces again, apparently having learned nothing from *Firefox*. In a sense, this is a way of avoiding the responsibility of having to strip off layers of character and get to the roots of personality. Instead Eastwood puts on characters, diverting the audience from his cool emotional range.

The film's white supremacist villains should be a militia army into big-time crime, but they emerge a cross between the fake revolutionaries of *The Enforcer* and the comic motorcycle gang of the Clyde movies. They practise with automatic weapons but turn into the ultimate gang that couldn't shoot straight. Having missed Clint with hundreds, if not thousands, of bullets, they then become the gang that can't even drive straight. The film ends with a damp squib, allowing Clint and Peters to head the pink Caddy into the sunset.

Verdict: 2/5

White Hunter, Black Heart (1990)

Crew: Director: Clint Eastwood, Executive Producer: David Valdes, Producer: Clint Eastwood (Warner Brothers/Malpaso), Screenplay: Peter Viertel, James Bridges, Burt Kennedy, Novel: Peter Viertel, Photography: Jack Green, Editor: Joel Cox, Music: Lennie Niehaus, Production Design: John Graysmark

Cast: Clint Eastwood (John Wilson), Jeff Fahey (Peter Verrill), Marisa Berenson (Kay Gibson), George Dzundza (Paul Landers), Richard Van-stone (Phil Duncan), Jamie Koss (Mrs Duncan), Timothy Spall (Hodkins), Boy Mathais Chuma (Kivu), Charlotte Cornwell (Mrs Wilding), Alun Armstrong (Lockheart), Mel Martin (Margaret McGregor), Clive Mantle (Harry)

Story: This is a thinly-disguised version of Peter Viertel's experiences with John Huston before the filming of *The African Queen*. John Wilson (i.e. Huston) is at war with producer Landers (Sam Spiegel) and wants to work on location to bag an elephant. He leaves for Africa with writer Verrill, where he has no time for the bigoted expatriate community, nor for the white hunter who forces him to let a huge tusker pass by because the situation is too dangerous. Wilson searches for the elephant with a new hunter and native guide Kivu. Even when shooting is scheduled to start, he takes advantage of the rain to resume his hunt. On the first day of filming, Kivu sights the tusker and Wilson leaves. He comes face to face with the elephant, but cannot shoot. As the elephant turns to leave, one of its young gets in the way; the elephant turns and charges. Kivu distracts it from Wilson and is killed. As the village begins to mourn, Wilson slumps into his director's chair and manages to order "Action."

Transformation: Wilson's Hemingway-esque philosophy of manhood and his own obsessions are transformed into tragic reality, and his film's ending is saved from false cynicism. Wilson is transformed from real hero to mere film director.

Background: *White Hunter, Black Heart* is so obviously based on John Huston that the temptation to judge it, and Clint's performance, on that basis distracts from its overall excellence. By ignoring most of the film business, and not making much of the Hepburn/Bogart/Bacall characters, Eastwood almost gets away from Huston. Almost, but not quite. It shouldn't matter. As a meditation on genius and control, and on our images of masculinity, this is Eastwood's most sombre film and his performance is certainly his most daring. Disguising himself with the speech and mannerisms of Huston freed him to explore farther than he would have otherwise. But Eastwood the actor always clutches that last bit of control.

The story is another *The Great Gatsby*, with Peter as Nick Carroway and Landers as Hyman Rothstein. It's also easy to read it as yet another essay in the travails of the independent director fighting against the studios. It's also one of the best Hemingway stories anyone has ever filmed. Wilson's combination of sensitivity and brusqueness, of ego and understanding, of con-man and bully, is played out by Eastwood as if he had been there.

Verdict: I like this film more each time I see it. 5/5

The Rookie (1990)

Crew: Director: Clint Eastwood, Producers: Howard Kanzanjian, Steven Siebert, David Valdes (Warner Brothers/Malpaso in association with Kazanjian/Siebert), Screenplay: Boaz Yakin, Scott Spiegel, Photography: Jack Green, Editor: Joel Cox, Music: Lennie Niehaus, Production Design: Judy Cammer, Second Unit Director: Buddy Van Horn, Stunts: Terry Leonard

Cast: Clint Eastwood (Nick Pulovski), Charlie Sheen (David Ackerman), Raul Julia (Strom), Sonia Braga (Liesl), Tom Skerrit (Eugene Ackerman), Lara Flynn Boyle (Sarah), Tony Plana (Morales), Marco Rodriquez (Loco), Mara Corday

Story: Nick gets saddled with rich kid David (haunted by the responsibility for his brother's death in childhood) after German car thief Strom and his gang kill his partner. Nick gets Morales to plant a bug, but Strom's partner Liesl kills him. The bug allows Nick to set up a trap, but David can't shoot Liesl and Nick is taken hostage. Later, Liesl has her way with the bound Nick. The city refuses to ransom Nick, so David gets the money from his father. His wife Sarah kills Loco, who had been waiting to kill David. David saves Nick; they chase the villains to the airport, and kill them.

Transformation: Nick goes from Daddy Harry to desk jockey, while white-collar David becomes Dirty Harry Junior.

Background: This is the most referential of the non-canonical Harry films: the city's refusal to ransom Nick inverts *Dirty Harry*; the female partner routine comes from *The Enforcer*; and the educated partner with second thoughts recalls the first two films.

One feels sympathy for critics' who claim Eastwood chooses star vehicles designed for specific purposes. In this case, he uses a young co-star to drag his image into the 1990s, appeal to a new audience and have an action hit after *Bird* and *White Hunter, Black Heart* failed at the box office. Although *The Rookie* took five times more in the US than Eastwood's previous film, it failed as a holiday blockbuster.

What you see is what you get. There are some good set piece stunts, lots of motorcycle fetishism and Lara Flynn Boyle, the Sean Young of the 1990s. She is arguably Eastwood's dumbest waif since Tobie, at least until she blows a villain away while watching *Tarantula* on TV! Even that isn't as weird as Julia and Braga playing German car thieves in LA – Braga's real role is like Vonetta McGee's: provide a sexy scene for the boss (and the scene is reprised from *Tightrope)*. Sexy as that may be, the effect is killed by the sight of her running through the airport in a jumpsuit.

Verdict: 2/5

Unforgiven (1992)

Crew: Director: Clint Eastwood, Executive Producer: David Valdes, Producer: Clint Eastwood (Warner Brothers/Malpaso), Screenplay: David Webb Peoples, Photography: Jack Green, Editor: Joel Cox, Music: Lennie Niehaus, Production Design: Henry Bumstead, Technical Consultant: Buddy Van Horn

Cast: Clint Eastwood (William Munny), Gene Hackman (Little Bill Daggett), Morgan Freeman (Ned Logan), Richard Harris (English Bob), Jaimz Woolvett (Schofield Kid), Saul Rubinek (Beauchamp), Anthony James (Skinny), Frances Fisher (Strawberry Alice), Anna Thomson (Delilah), Beverly Elliott (Silky), Tara Dawn Frederick (Little Sue)

Story: Whores in Big Whiskey, Wyoming, put a bounty on two cowboys, one of whom slashed a whore who laughed at his pecker. Daggett makes the cowboys compensate the saloon owner for the whore's lost business. William Munny, a former thief and murderer, widowed and raising two children on a hog farm, is approached by the Schofield Kid to chase the bounty. He recruits his reluctant old partner Logan. Meanwhile, Daggett wants no bounty hunters; he runs off English Bob, whose dime novel biographer stays to write about Daggett. Daggett beats Munny and drives him off – the others escape with the aid of the whores. Munny kills one of the cowboys with Ned's rifle. Ned loses his stomach for killing and heads home, but is captured and tortured to death by Daggett. Schofield kills the other cowboy and he and Munny learn of Ned's death when claiming their bounty. Munny rides into Big Whiskey, kills the saloon owner who is displaying Ned's body, then kills Daggett and his deputies. He leaves town. A caption tells us he is rumoured to have become successful in dry goods in San Francisco.

Transformation: While Schofield and Ned discover they are no longer killers, Munny's redemption ends when the mythic killer inside him is reborn.

Background: This is a wonderful Western, which picks up added resonance from the way it draws on Eastwood's cowboy past. If *Heartbreak Ridge* was about playing John Wayne, *Unforgiven* is about playing The Man With No Name. This film simply would not work without the baggage Clint brings to it. It is as good a use of a star's resonance as any director has managed, and a true measure of Clint's awareness. (Clint optioned, bought and sat on the screenplay for more than a decade, waiting until he was right for the role.)

Is the whores' vengeance the film's motivation? Delilah is visibly touched by the cowboy's kindness when he brings her a pony, but her colleagues drive him away, ensuring his death. The attack on Delilah takes on the aspects of a modern sex crime, producing a puzzled response from men who are dedicated killers themselves, but can't understand mutilating a whore. But all this is secondary to Munny's rebirth.

The film gains power by delaying Munny's transformation. This is an ensemble film. As long as there is an ulterior motive to Munny's journey: getting the bounty, he remains part of the ensemble. His scenes are dominated by Ned and the Schofield Kid, while Daggett and Bob supply the film's fireworks. Once Munny's purpose is reduced to pure killing, vengeance and death, Clint returns to the character he started his career playing. It is as if that character had spent the ensuing decades doing nothing but "being lucky at killing folks." He takes command of the screen, like a cavalry charge, perfectly measured, timed and weighted.

The references to classic Western myth adds resonance. Little Bill's house, a symbol of civilisation taming the west, is lopsided and leaky, visibly flawed. The dime writer, a stock character from many classic 1950s Westerns, reminds us of how false our myths are, even as Munny convinces us yet again they can be real. And the ending, with Munny vanishing into prosperity at the end of the Western line (California), brings three centuries of American Western myth to a close.

Verdict: A classic. In the past twenty years, Hollywood has doled out best director Oscars to actors with unseemly generosity. This one is fully deserved, probably the most deserved best film Oscar of the 1990s. 5/5

Fifth Cycle: Grand Old Man

Following the success of *Unforgiven*, Clint's status was cemented. As a director, he had created a commercial and artistic success, finally merging both strands of his long career. As an actor, he had given The Man With No Name a final farewell, and signalled an openness which promised a wider range of characters...

In The Line Of Fire (1993)

Crew: Director: Wolfgang Peterson, Executive Producers: Wolfgang Peterson, Gail Katz, David Valdes, Producer: Jeff Apple (Castle Rock/Columbia), Screenplay: Jeff Maguire, Photography: John Bailey, Music: Ennio Morricone, Editors: Anne V Coates, Steven Kemper, Production Design: Lilly Kilvert, Stunts: Buddy Van Horn

Cast: Clint Eastwood (Frank Horrigan) John Malkovich (Mitch Leary), Rene Russo (Lilly Raines), Dylan McDermott (Al D'Andrea), Gary Cole (Bill Watts), John Mahoney (Sam Campagna), Fred Thompson (Harry Sargeant), John Heard (Professor Riger), Clyde Kuhatsu (Jack), Jim Curley (President)

Story: Horrigan is the last man left from the detail that 'lost' JFK in Dallas. He discovers a potential assassin, 'Booth' who appears to be obsessed with Horrigan. Because of Booth's interest and despite his age and the objections of bureaucrat Watts, Horrigan is returned to duty on the President's protection team. Horrigan meets new colleague Lilly Raines, who is attracted to him despite his dinosaur demeanour. Horrigan gets Booth's prints after a chase, but the CIA withhold his identity. After mistakenly sounding the alarm during a speech (Booth popped a balloon), Horrigan forces the CIA to reveal that Booth is CIA assassin Mitch Leary. After another chase, Horrigan's partner is killed and Leary saves Horrigan's life. In LA, after bracing an innocent waiter in front of the TV cameras, Horrigan is demoted to advance work in San Diego, but stumbles on the connection which allows him to identify Leary as a guest at the LA banquet. He races back to LA, takes a bullet meant for the President and wins a fight with Leary in an elevator. Rather than let Horrigan save him, Leary plunges to his death. Horrigan retires, but gets Lilly.

Background: Imagine if Harry Callahan's life had been defined by one huge failure, like Scorpio killing all the kids on the school bus and escaping, then he might be Frank Horrigan. This film can also be seen as Clint's answer to Oliver Stone's *JFK*. In its most moving sequence, Horrigan explains to Lilly about the day of the assassination, and his failure to take the bullet meant for the President. He shrugs off with disgust all the various conspiracy theories ("idiots on bar stools") – all that really matters in Horrigan's world is that he failed in his job, as a hero, to save John Kennedy. This is as close as Clint comes to crying until *The Bridges Of Madison County*. Yet the film appears to share with *JFK* the idea that America has gone off the rails since the assassination; Horrigan's failure deprived America of its last heroic President. (Note that Horrigan's protests against conspiracy theories come in a movie where a CIA assassin is aiming to kill the President for revenge against the agency, who hide his identity from the Secret Service.) Yet Horrigan also takes the side of war protesters over Nixon's chief of staff in an argument with soon-to-be-Senator-for-real Fred Thompson.

One of Leary's many disguises in the film (none of which hide the fact that he is John Malkovich, any more than Clint's did in *Firefox*) is your basic Vietnam veteran psycho. Significantly, this is the first disguise Horrigan sees through. The film revolves around disguise, opening with Horrigan pretending to be a counterfeiter. Leary's light reading is a magazine called *New Age Modeler* and as he disguises himself director Petersen morphs his face in a way that echoes police identikit models. Horrigan, whose control masks the pain of his past failure, drops his mask for Lilly in one of Eastwood's best scenes. No, he doesn't actually cry, but the suggestion of tears is as strong as anything he's done to this point. It came in his first film since *Escape From Alcatraz* with an established director.

Verdict: Superior formula thriller, helped by an excellent Ennio Morricone score. 4/5

A Perfect World (1993)

Crew: Director: Clint Eastwood, Producer: Marc Johnson, David Valdes, Screenplay: John Lee Hancock, Photography: Jack Green, Editors: Joel Cox, Ron Spang, Music: Lennie Niehaus, Production Design: Henry Bumstead, Stunts: Buddy Van Horn

Cast: Kevin Costner (Butch Haynes), Clint Eastwood (Red Garnett), Laura Dern (Sally Gerber), TJ Lowther (Philip Perry), Leo Burmester (Tom), Paul Hewitt (Dick), Bradley Whitford (Bobby Lee), Keith Szarabajka (Terry), Jennifer Griffin (Momma), Darryl Cox (Mr Hughes), Dennis Letts (Governor), George Orrison (Officer Orrison)

Story: Butch and Terry, escaped from jail, are stealing a car when Terry breaks in on Phillip's mom, attacking her. Butch stops him but they take Philip hostage. When Terry tries to abuse Philip, Butch kills him. Meanwhile, Texas Ranger Garnett commandeers the Governor's campaign mobile home to lead the hunt, accompanied by FBI sniper Bobby Lee and criminologist Sally. Butch and Philip hit the road for Alaska, from which

Butch's absentee father once sent him a postcard, which he still carries. Sally wins Garnett's respect, and learns he was responsible for Butch being sent to a tough reform school for joyriding. Garnett thought getting Butch away from his criminal father would be better for him. Butch and Philip accept the hospitality of a black sharecropper, Mack. When Mack hits his son, an incensed Butch prepares to shoot him, but Philip shoots Butch instead. Severely wounded, Butch tracks down a frightened Philip in a field. The police arrive and Garnett tries to end the stand-off. As Butch reaches to give Philip his prized postcard, Bobby Lee kills him.

Transformations: Garnett is transformed from know-it-all to know-nothing.

Background: This is a film about fathers who, in a perfect world, stay with their sons and give them love. Butch is failed by both his real father and his symbolic father, Garnett. He is also a liberating father figure to Philip, who kills him when he demonstrates his own cruelty.

Costner is understated throughout and at his very best when he suddenly snaps and turns psychopathic when he sees a father strike his son – it is a shrewd use of Costner's limitations by a director more aware than most how less is more. But Costner's death scene slows the film at just the point it should be picking up. The idea is to draw out the tension. Will the sniper get him or won't he? But the reality is that we see a catalogue of reaction shots, and this dissipates much of the energy Costner has built up. He also jumps back from a psychopath to the soppy Costner we know and love.

Set just before the 1963 Kennedy assassination, designer Bumstead and cinematographer Green create a Norman Rockwell-esque environment. It is a reminder of a different way of life and an idealised perception of childhood.

Verdict: The strengths outdo the weaknesses. 4/5

The Bridges Of Madison County (1995)

Crew: Director: Clint Eastwood, Producers: Clint Eastwood, Kathleen Kennedy (Warner Brothers/Malpaso), Screenplay: Richard LaGravenese, Novel: Robert James Waller, Photography: Jack Green, Editor: Joel Cox, Music: Lennie Niehaus

Cast: Clint Eastwood (Robert Kincaid), Meryl Streep (Francesca Johnson), Annie Corley (Carolyn), Victor Slezak (Michael), Jim Haynie (Richard), Sarah Kathryn Schmitt (Young Carolyn), Christopher Kroon (Young Michael)

Story: Wondering why their mother wants her ashes scattered over a bridge, her children uncover her diary. They learn the story of her four-day affair with photographer Kincaid, there to shoot the eponymous bridges.

Although she chose to stay with her family, the two were the loves of each others' lives, and Kincaid's ashes are already scattered at the same bridge, where they met.

Background: The fact that Clint's version is so much superior to the best-selling book is a reminder of just how bad the original was. By switching the focus to Francesca's life, recognising her choice as the key moment of the film, Eastwood not only creates a tension the book lacked, but places himself, as star, in the perfect position to let Streep, the actress, play out her dilemma. He uses his star quality to make himself the sex object in a way he hasn't been since *Play Misty For Me*.

The beauty of this film, beyond the understated nature of true love, is the careful way it is composed as a *National Geographic* photographer might. It is full of internal frames for scenes. It plays with the way photographs suggest memory and conveys a sense of huge stillness which refers back to the classic Eastwood landscape.

Shooting took place where the book is set, in Winterset, Iowa, which is also the birthplace of John Wayne. The film was a co-production with Steven Spielberg's Amblin, and Richard Combs points out that, as in all Amblin movies, the family always triumphs. Eastwood's take on the relationship was more revealing, "Reality sets in, whether it's a week later, a year, or ten years, eventually they'd hate each other. She'd always regret leaving her children." Clint saw it more as an on-location romance, even if one of unusual depth and intensity, of the type common to Hollywood stars.

The silent farewell scene is one of the most daring of Eastwood's career. Kincaid stands soaked and literally washed out by the rain, emotionally draining as we watch, no longer a sex object, all glamour removed from his image. It is also a cautious scene. Does he cry? Earlier, he turned away from the camera and hid his tears. Now raindrops will hide his teardrops and no one will ever know.

Verdict: Tears or no, this not-so-*Brief Encounter* is one of Eastwood's best. 4/5

Completists note: Clint played himself in a cameo, in *Casper* (1995) directed by Brad Siberling. Considering all the Casper product placement in *A Perfect World*, it probably made sense.

Absolute Power (1996)

Crew: Director: Clint Eastwood, Executive Producer: Tom Rooker, Producers: Clint Eastwood, Karen Spiegel (Castle Rock/Malpaso), Screenplay: William Goldman, Novel: David Baldacci, Photography: Jack Green, Editor: Joel Cox, Music: Lennie Niehaus, Production Design: Henry Bumstead, Stunts: Buddy Van Horn

Cast: Clint Eastwood (Luther Whitney), Gene Hackman (President Richmond), Ed Harris (Detective Seth Frank), Laura Linney (Kate Whitney), EG Marshall (Walter Sullivan), Judy Davis (Gloria Russell), Scott Glenn (Agent Burton), Dennis Haysbert (Agent Collins), Alison Eastwood (Art Student), Kimber Eastwood (White House Guide)

Story: Burglar Whitney breaks into the house of wealthy power-broker Sullivan. Unexpectedly, Sullivan's young wife Christy turns up, with President Richmond. As Whitney watches behind a one-way mirror in a concealed vault, their love-making turns violent. Two secret service agents burst in and kill Christy. Chief of Staff Gloria Russell engineers a cover-up, but leaves behind a bloody letter opener with which Christy stabbed the President. Whitney escapes and, intending to skip the country, tries to patch things up with his estranged daughter, Kate. However, at the airport he is so disgusted by Richmond's sanctimony that he changes his mind and sends a note to Russell. Detective Frank is convinced Whitney is involved, and persuades Kate to arrange a meeting with her father. When Whitney shows up, so do the guilty secret service agents and an assassin hired by Sullivan to kill Whitney. The agents try to kill Kate by pushing her car over a cliff. Whitney kills one agent at the hospital when he tries to finish the job. He gets to Sullivan and tells him the real story. Sullivan visits the President, carrying the letter opener. Later the President's suicide is announced, Russell is arrested, Whitney and Kate are reconciled and Frank and Kate are OK to start dating.

Transformation: Whitney from burglar to family man (he even gives back Sullivan's family jewels, symbolically freeing him to reclaim his manhood by assassinating a President).

Background: Continuing Eastwood's run of movies based on best-sellers, the film version of *Absolute Power* marked Clint's first opportunity to work with top-of-the-line screenwriter William Goldman, who was forced to re-adapt his original script to keep Whitney alive. In the novel, his daughter's betrayal leads to his death; grief and guilt-stricken, she combines with Seth Frank to bring the guilty, including the President, to justice. That version packs more emotional charge (and leaves Ed Harris feeling less like a teenager) but of course it takes the star out of the film halfway through, and no one's buying tickets to see Laura Linney ice secret service agents (though maybe they should be). Some sexual material was also lost, particularly between the President and his chief of staff Russell. This has the dual effect of making the scene where she thinks he's given her a necklace merely comic, and also of losing the obvious parallel between her character and Hillary Clinton. Interestingly, when the President starts to get down with Christy, the music is right out of *Play Misty For Me*.

In many ways, Clint is a perfect director for the star-laden best-seller vehicle. He has a super cast, with EG Marshall stealing as much of the show as he is allowed to (in his first role with Hackman since an episode of *The Defender*s in the early 1960s) and virtually every scene crackling as high-powered talents are given space to play their characters, even when those roles are relatively small.

It's not far-fetched to see this as Clint's most overtly political film. Whitney's snarling disgust at the hypocrisy of President Richmond (Richmond, capital of the Confederacy, equals Southerner, read President Bubba Bill Clinton) might seem risky coming from a man whose own marital track record is somewhat spotty, but we can take the implication that a real-life Bill Clinton Eastwood would at least look after his daughter while being an absentee father, save her life when required, or, like director Eastwood, give her acting jobs (two daughters on this film!).

In Whitney's safe house, the literal safe is a Monticello (reminding us of a different kind of President from the South) and Whitney's steamer trunks are emblazoned with "proud supporter of Desert Storm" stickers. Yet the implication that America is going down the tubes because of a libidinous, insincere politician doesn't gel with the vision of a monied, perverse king-maker, who orders killings and murders a President with impunity, nor with a secret service that seem to have turned into the Gestapo since Frank Horrigan retired.

Verdict: Decent, but uninspiring, blockbuster. Compare Clint's pacing with Petersen's in *In The Line of Fire*. 3/5

Midnight In The Garden Of Good And Evil (1997)

Crew: Director: Clint Eastwood, Producers: Clint Eastwood, Arnold Stiefel (Warner Brothers/Malpaso with Silver Films), Screenplay: John Lee Hancock, Book: John Berendt, Photography: Jack Green, Editor: Joel Cox, Music: Lennie Niehaus, Production Design: Henry Bumstead

Cast: Kevin Spacey (Jim Williams), John Cusack (John Kelso), Jack Thompson (Sonny Seiler), Jude Law (Billy Hanson), The Lady Chablis (Herself), Alison Eastwood (Mandy Nichols), Irma P Hall (Minerva), Paul

Hipp (Joe Odom), Anne Haney (Margaret Williams), Geoffrey Lewis (Luther), Sonny Seiler (Judge White)

Story: Journalist John Kelso arrives in Savannah, Georgia, to cover Jim Williams' annual Christmas party for *Town & Country* magazine. On the night of the party Williams kills his handyman/lover Billy Hanson, a local rent boy drug dealer. Kelso stays to write a book about the trial, making a deal for access with Williams (who pleads self-defence), and his good ol' boy lawyer Sonny. Kelso finds himself more and more attracted to the guignol charms of Savannah and to Williams' neighbour Mandy Nichols. Aided by her and drag queen Chablis, he uncovers evidence that helps exonerate Williams but, before he does, Williams fabricates another story which implies the shooting may not have been self-defence. Williams is acquitted, but dies of a heart attack, which voodoo priestess Minerva may have helped Hanson engineer from beyond the grave. Provoked by Minerva into accepting Mandy's love, Kelso finds himself unable to leave Savannah.

Transformation: Kelso should be transformed by the outré charms of Savannah but the film fails to take that route.

Background: On the simplest level, Clint reworks the best-selling memoir as a courtroom drama, in which journalist John Kelso gets to find the key clue, free Jim Williams (who is more likely guilty than not) and be seduced by the charms of Mandy Nichols. The problem is that the real story, which is scratching to get out, should be the seduction of Kelso by Savannah's decadent lifestyle, if not by the personality and style of Williams. Where the book lost its impetus as the trial scenes dragged on, here the film gains excitement, especially with Jack Thompson reprising his *Breaker Morant* role as the country lawyer who's sharper than he acts.

The real problem is that Kelso, and Clint, don't trust decadence very much, so they keep the audience at a distance from it. The leisurely pace would work better if we, and Kelso, found the steamy world of Savannah more and more exotic. In Clint's hands the local exotica becomes relatively benign, and Kelso's reaction is generally tired bemusement. The most obvious example is Chablis, playing herself. Clint obviously loves his/her performance, and she is given the film's best set pieces, but she is a bird in a gilded cage and not part of a natural landscape.

A better way to consider *Midnight In The Garden Of Good And Evil* is as a redoing of *The Beguiled*. Again, a wounded northerner (Kelso's failed book led to a failed marriage, and boy is he scarred) is taken into a gothic mansion under suspicion (after the killing his presence is first deemed dangerous). We reprise *The Beguiled*'s key quartet of Clint's female archetypes: his daughter Alison plays the waif, while Chablis is the whore (ironic, since she is literally a wannabe woman). There are two wise old women, Minerva and Margaret Williams. The former recalls the slave Hallie, and the latter's silence may be taken as a reaction to the perversion of her son. Finally, the wannabe man, the would-be equal and seducer is Jim Williams. Kelso must make his own choice, just as McBurney did, but note that he consummates his relationship with Mandy only after he discovers Williams has lied to him. (The relationship disappears until the film's end.) If Kelso had already been seduced by Savannah, this revelation of lies would carry far more power. Now he merely settles for a rather blowsy version of the waif.

Verdict: 2/5

True Crime (1999)

Crew: Director: Clint Eastwood, Executive Producer: Tom Rooker, Producers: Clint Eastwood, Richard D Zanuck, Lili Fini Zanuck (Warner Brothers/Zanuck/Malpaso), Screenplay: Larry Gross, Paul Brickman, Stephen Schiff, Novel: Andrew Klavan, Photography: Jack Green, Editor: Joel Cox, Music: Lennie Niehaus, Production Design: Henry Bumstead, Stunts: Buddy Van Horn

Cast: Clint Eastwood ('Ev' Everett), Isaiah Washington (Frank Beechum), Denis Leary (Bob Findley), Lisa Gay Hamilton (Bonnie Beechum), Diane Venora (Barbara Everett), James Woods (Alan Mann), Bernard Hill (Warden), Mary McCormack (Michelle), Laila Robbins (Patricia Findley), Hattie Winston (Mrs Russel), Frances Fisher, William Windom, Francesa Frances Fisher (Celia), Dina Eastwood (Wilma), Lucy Alexis Liu, Anthony Zerbe (Governor)

Story: When his colleague Michelle is killed in a road crash (after turning down his proposition) reporter Ev, a womaniser with drinking and family problems, takes over her assignment, interviewing Frank Beechum before his execution for the murder of a convenience store clerk. Ev becomes convinced Beechum is innocent, and discovers the prosecutors knew of a witness who left the store moments before the killing. Ev breaks into Michelle's apartment, finds the name of the witness, tracks down the witness' grandmother and discovers that he is dead. Drowning his sorrows, Ev sees a report on the news, and recognises on the murdered girl a charm he's seen on the witness' grandmother's neck. He drives the grandmother to the home of his publisher, who calls the governor and stays the execution. A year later, Beechum spends Christmas with his family, while Ev is alone.

Transformation: Ev is another William Munny character, but this one has to lose his family before he can become a good reporter again.

Background: There isn't much of a thriller here, because both the mechanical nature of the plot (Ev doesn't solve the crime as much as realise

Michelle actually was a pretty good reporter) and the direction (Clint tells the audience in advance that the grandmother's locket is important) let it down. It's also awkward because Clint is at least 15 and probably more like 25 years too old for the role, which requires his propositioning women in their 20s to be believable. This may work for the real Eastwood, but the Ev character lacks his Hollywood appeal. This is emphasised even more by the way the scenes of Ev with his family look more like Luther Whitney with his daughter, if she and Detective Frank had a baby.

The newsroom scenes work, with James Woods at his over-the-top best as an old style editor, playing nicely off Denis Leary's obnoxious bottom-line modern executive. That Ev is sleeping with Leary's wife (again the age question raises its head) adds an almost comic dimension, which indicates one of many different roads this film might've travelled.

The urban scenes are straight out of *Dirty Harry*, though I hesitate to add Ev to the list of pseudo-Harrys. Still, Clint's opening bar scene with Mary McCormack could be right out of *Play Misty For Me*. Most of the urban scenes are set during night, and have a darkness shared by the prison. These are contrasted nicely with the very bright, clinical and antiseptic newsroom (similar to the courtroom and hospital in *Midnight In The Garden Of Good And Evil*, but without the made-for-TV movie lighting). Interestingly, Ev's family scene is shot to keep sunlight out and establish his home as another prison.

Verdict: In the end, a film as tired as Ev. 2/5

Space Cowboys (2000)

Crew: Director: Clint Eastwood, Executive Producer: Tom Rooker, Producers: Clint Eastwood, Andrew Lazar (Warner Brothers/Village Roadshow/Clipsal/Malpaso/Mad Chance), Screenplay: Ken Kaufman, Howard Klausner, Photography: Jack Green, Editor: Joel Cox, Music: Lennie Niehaus, Production Design: Henry Bumstead

Cast: Clint Eastwood (Frank Corvin), Tommy Lee Jones (Hawk Hawkins), Donald Sutherland (Jerry O'Neill), James Garner (Tank Sullivan), James Cromwell (General Gerson), Marcia Gay Harden (Sara Holland), William Devane (Eugene Davis), Loren Dean (Ethan), Courtney B Vance (Roger), Rade Sherbedgia (Vostov), Barbara Babcock (Barbara Corvin), Blair Brown (Dr Caruthers)

Story: The Daedalus team of test pilots led by Frank Corvin, removed from the space programme after a 1958 crash, are reunited, over the objections of General Gerson, to fix a Russian communications satellite which is falling out of orbit. Following his fitness exam, Hawkins learns he has terminal cancer. In space, the team discover the satellite contains six nuclear missiles, fail-safe targeted at US cities. Astronaut Grace, assigned to the mission at Gerson's insistence, ignores Corvin's orders, accidentally activates the missiles and damages the shuttle. Corvin and Hawkins manage to recapture the satellite but to get them out of Earth's orbit Hawkins volunteers to pilot the launch platform towards the moon. He succeeds, and Frank brings the shuttle back safely to Earth.

Transformation: A Munny-esque return to youthful prowess, though the most poignant transformation is Hawkins' from frustrated astronaut to moon rock.

Background: When we first see the young actors playing Clint and Tommy Lee Jones in the 1958 scenes, we are struck by how blandly attractive they seem, cut from that straight-edged television mould. Then we realise that this is pretty much what Clint Eastwood looked like in 1958, on the verge of his *Rawhide* days, after his spell as potential beefcake at Universal. It's instructive to see just how far Clint (and James Garner, for that matter) have come since those television days.

This film is a meditation on ageing but Clint, as ever, is not particularly meditative. Although everyone they know appears to have died, Clint and his Three Musketeers seem undaunted, except in inconsequential ways, by age. Anyway, NASA's requirements are so lax James Garner gets into space without being able to run 20 yards! James Cromwell returns (after *Pink Cadillac*) as a prototype bureaucratic arsehole, but his more heinous villainy is telegraphed far too early and often. On the positive side, Jones plays a wonderful scene with Harden, explaining his affection for an old experimental jet, which only performed well when it was at the speed and altitude it was designed for. As a metaphor for Eastwood, one could do worse.

Clint shies away from one last risk. For all the beauty of seeing Earth reflected in Hawkins' helmet on the moon, the film might end better with Frank and his wife looking at the moon, wondering whether Hawkins did get there, rather than assuring the audience he did.

Verdict: It would be better with a sharper edge, but the cast and good feeling carry it. I'm not sure if the word 'Cowboys' in the title indicates another cycle has been completed. 3/5

Conclusion

Also in 2000, Clint directed the music video *Why Should I Care?* for the pianist/singer Diana Krall. This led to their being linked romantically, which both denied convincingly.

Blood Work was scheduled to begin filming in autumn 2001. It is an adaptation of Michael Connelly's novel, in which FBI profiler Terry McCaleb receives a life-saving heart transplant, only to discover that there was more to the heart's becoming available than meets the eye. Connelly's use of this transformation to cue further changes in McCaleb fits right into the Eastwood canon. However, McCaleb is considerably younger than Eastwood and there is a romantic sub-plot involving the single-parent sister of the organ donor, which would require some modification for Clint to play it. The screenplay is by Brian Helgeland (*LA Confidential*, *Payback*), who has been rumoured at times to direct.

Eastwood bought an early draft of the book. When he met with the author he suggested two changes. One was to eliminate the villain's flight to Mexico, which Connelly says he ignored. "Maybe it would work in a movie that the bad guy would not try to escape from LA or even the country but I don't think I could get away with that in a book. I think Clint was looking at the expense of shooting in two places. I didn't have to worry about that in a book."

Connelly took Eastwood's other piece of advice, which was to raise the stakes at the end. "So I made changes, the most significant being the bad guy kidnapped Graciela and the boy. I thought it was good advice that's why I put his name in the acknowledgements."

Blood Work could be sharper and darker than *True Crime*. Connelly is a writer remarkably free of sentiment, which is a good place to start.

And where does Clint go from there? "I always thought *Unforgiven* was sort of a perfect last Western," he said. "But I'd do another if I could find the right one."

James Fenimore Cooper's *The Prairie* comes to mind, where the geriatric Hawkeye and Chingnachook head into the sunset. Yes, he's already done it in *The Outlaw Josey Wales* and *Unforgiven*, but as an epic it suggests myriad possibilities.

Whatever he does, his place in film history is already sure. Years ago Clint said, "If there's one thing I learned from Don Siegel, it's to know what you want to shoot, and to know what you're seeing when you see it." That's actually two things. Clint has established himself as a master of the second, and through a long career has steadily improved his sense of the first. Perhaps all that's left to see is what happens when the control implicit in that knowing is relaxed just a little more. Could it get better? We could only hope.

Reference Materials

Books

The incredible amount of material published about Eastwood ranges from totally tabloid to numbingly academic. It's probably best to start with the two full-scale biographies. Richard Schickel's *Clint Eastwood* (1996) is an authorised version and thus limited (one critic says Schickel plays 'Ruskin to Eastwood's Turner'). It does have a few fine critical insights. Patrick McGilligan's *Clint: The Life And Legend* (HarperCollins, 1999) thinks of itself as brandishing the sword of truth, but has its own problems. McGilligan uncovers much about Eastwood's private life, seemingly aimed at proving Eastwood a hypocrite, as if it somehow downgrades his on-screen work. When Eastwood occasionally appears to hold others to moral standards he fails to meet, fair enough, but McGilligan constantly judges Clint by an impossible double standard, expecting him to live up to his screen image. He also attributes persistently artistic decisions to character flaws (for example, Clint's films are dark because he's too cheap to pay for more lights). His most cogent critical points rarely lead him to the obvious conclusions, but the two books complement each other nicely, if you're willing to indulge some 1200 pages. A slighter, more entertaining picture comes from Stuart M Kaminsky's *Clint Eastwood* (Signet, 1974) which is especially good on the Siegel/Eastwood relationship, not surprising since Kaminsky also authored *Don Siegel, Director* (Curtis, 1974), which is equally entertaining in its 1970s way.

The best of the critical studies is Edward Gallafant's *Clint Eastwood: Actor And Director* (Studio Vista, 1994). I also found Daniel O'Brien's *Clint Eastwood, Film-Maker* (Batsford, 1996) straightforward, even if I questioned some of the judgements. *Clint Eastwood Interviews* (eds Robert Kapsis & Kathie Coblentz, Mississippi University, 1999) is a very useful collection. Also interesting are *Clint Eastwood: A Cultural Production* by Paul Smith (University of Minnesota, 1993) and *Clint Eastwood: Hollywood's Loner* by Michael Munn (Robson, 1992). Also consulted were: *Clint Eastwood: Movin On* by Peter Douglas (Henry Regnery, 1974), *Clint Eastwood* by François Guérif (Henri Veyrier, 1982), *Clint Eastwood: The Man Behind The Myth* by Patrick Agar (Robert Hale 1975), *Clint Eastwood* by Gerald Cole and Peter Williams (WH Allen, 1983), *The Films Of Clint Eastwood* by Boris Zmijewsky & Lee Pfeiffer (Citadel, 1982, since revised) and *Clint Eastwood, Sexual Cowboy* by Douglas Thompson (Smith,Gryphon, 1992). Each contains something of value, even the last.

Christopher Frayling's *Sergio Leone* (Faber & Faber, 2000) and *Spaghetti Westerns* (IB Tauris, 1999) are invaluable. Readers might also like to check out my own *Sergio Leone* (Pocket Essentials, 2001) which features a more comprehensive bibliography on Leone and Westerns, Spaghetti and otherwise.

A Siegel Film by Don Siegel (Faber & Faber, 1993) is a revealing autobiography of Siegel's films. Also worthwhile is Alan Lovell's *Don Siegel, American Cinema* (BFI, 1975). Peter Bogdanovich's 1968 take on Siegel in *Who The Devil Made It* (Ballantine, 1998) holds up still. David Thomson's *Biographical Dictionary Of Film* (Andre Deutsch, 1994) entries on Eastwood and Siegel are excellent, as are Kim Newman's essays on *Dirty Harry* and *Coogan's Bluff* in the *BFI Companion To Crime* (ed Phil Hardy, Cassell, 1997).

The BFI Companion To The Western (ed Edward Buscombe, MOMI, 1991) remains a first port of call. *The Western Reader* (eds Jim Kitses & Greg Rickman, Limelight, 1998) includes a 1992 interview with Eastwood by Kenneth Turan and an interesting essay on masculinity in *Unforgiven* by Janet Thumim, while *The Movie Book Of The Western* (eds Ian Cameron & Douglas Pye, Studio Vista, 1996) has Leighton Grist's essay on *Unforgiven*.

As always, I was reminded on how much I learned from two teachers when I consulted Richard Slotkin's *Gunfighter Nation* (Atheneum, 1992) and Jeanine Basinger's *The World War II Combat Film* (Columbia University, 1986).

Articles

There are hundreds, many recycled through the biographies and studies. Among the best of those used were:

Peter Biskind, 'Any Which Way He Can' *Premiere*, April 1993

Tim Cahill, 'Rolling Stone Interview' *Rolling Stone* 4 July 1985

Richard Combs, 'Shadowing The Hero' *Sight & Sound*, October 1992

Richard Combs, 'Old Ghosts' *Film Comment*, May/June 1996

Lem Dobbs, 'Homage To Peckinpah' *Sight & Sound*, October 1992

Ginny Dougary, 'His Own Man' *Time*, 28 March 1998

Clint Eastwood, 'Don Siegel, The Padron' *Film Comment*, September/October 1991

Philip French, 'Guns' *Sight & Sound*, Spring 1974

Pierre Greenfield, 'Dirty Dogs, Dirty Devils, And Dirty Harry' *Velvet Light Trap* 16, Fall 1978

J Hoberman, 'How The Western Was Lost' *Village Voice*, 27 August 1991

Jay Holben, 'Great Relationships: Eastwood & Jack Green' *American Cinematographer*, November 1998

Barbara Isenberg, 'True Clint' *Modern Maturity*, March/April 2001

Karyn Kay, 'The Beguiled: Gothic Misogyny' *Velvet Light Trap* 16, Fall 1978

Peter Keough, 'Ghostly Presences' *Sight & Sound*, October 1992

Dick Lochte, 'Clint Eastwood On Clint Eastwood' *Los Angeles Free Press*, 20 April 1973

Todd McCarthy, 'Hollywood Style '84: Bruce Surtees' *Film Comment*, March/April 1984

Robert Mazzocco, 'The Supply Side Star' *New York Review of Books*, 1 April 1982

David Meeker, 'Lennie Niehaus, Cherokee To Madison County' *Sight & Sound*, September 1995

Kathleen Murphy, 'The Good, The Bad, And The Ugly' *Film Comment*, May/June 1996

Andrew Sarris, 'Don Siegel: The Pro' *Film Comment*, September/October 1991

Harry Sheehan, 'Dark Worlds' *Sight & Sound*, June 1991

David Thomson, 'Cop On A Hot Tightrope' *Film Comment*, September/October 1984

Amy Taubin, 'An Upright Man' *Sight & Sound*, September 1993

James Verniere, 'Stepping Out' *Sight & Sound*, September 1993

Videos & DVDs

Eastwood's entire filmography is available, though sometimes only in Area 1 DVD and NTSC VHS (USA formats). The following films are available only in VHS: *Any Which Way You Can, City Heat, Coogan's Bluff, The Dead Pool, The Enforcer, Every Which Way You Can, Firefox, Heartbreak Ridge, Honkytonk Man, Lafayette Escadrille, In The Line Of Fire, Magnum Force, A Perfect World, Pink Cadillac, Revenge Of The Creature, The Rookie, Sudden Impact, Tarantula, Tightrope, Two Mules For Sister Sara, Where Eagles Dare.* There appears to be a critical judgement involved here! Eastwood's AFI Tribute show is also available.

Television

The 2000 PBS American Masters programme produced by Bruce Ricker and Dave Kehr (shown on BBC *Arena*) is excellent. Almost as interesting is Gene Feldman's 1993 *Man From Malpaso*, which reflects the then-recent success of *Unforgiven* and includes revealing interviews with many of the company. Henry Bumstead is particularly lucid: "It's no-bullshit film-making." The 1995 *South Bank Show* produced by Gerald Fox covers Eastwood's formative years. The 1993 AFI Tribute show is what one would expect, but gives a fair overview. Derek Malcolm's 1995 *Guardian Interview* at the NFT displays Clint's considerable reticence, but benefits from some sharp questions from the crowd.

Howard Hill's *Once Upon A Time: Sergio Leone* (Channel 4, 2001) is a welcome complement to the BBC's *Viva Leone*, produced by Nick Freund Jones in 1989.

Internet

There are many Eastwood pages out there, but two sites are of note:

ClintEastwood.net (www.clinteastwood.net) has lots of multimedia features, a good filmography, links to other sites and video/DVD purchase.

Clint Eastwood Page (www.localsonly.wilmington.net/~solomon/clinteastwood.html) also has in-depth coverage.

The site for PBS' American Masters features an essay by writer David Kehr and an interview with Eastwood and producer Bruce Ricker (www.pbs.org/wnet/americanmasters/database/eastwood_c.html)

The Sergio Leone homepage is excellent: (www.film.tierranet.com/directors/s.leone/sergioleone/html)

The Essential Library: Currently Available

Film Directors:

Woody Allen (Revised)	**Tim Burton**	**Ang Lee**
Jane Campion (£2.99)	**John Carpenter**	**Steve Soderbergh**
Jackie Chan	**Joel & Ethan Coen**	**Clint Eastwood**
David Cronenberg	**Terry Gilliam** (£2.99)	
Alfred Hitchcock	**Krzysztof Kieslowski** (£2.99)	
Stanley Kubrick	**Sergio Leone**	
David Lynch	**Brian De Palma** (£2.99)	
Sam Peckinpah (£2.99)	**Ridley Scott**	
Orson Welles	**Billy Wilder**	
Steven Spielberg	**Mike Hodges**	

Film Genres:

Film Noir	**Hong Kong Heroic Bloodshed** (£2.99)
Horror Films	**Slasher Movies**
Spaghetti Westerns	**Vampire Films** (£2.99)
Blaxploitation Films	**Bollywood**
French New Wave	

Film Subjects:

Laurel & Hardy	**Marx Brothers**
Steve McQueen (£2.99)	**Marilyn Monroe**
The Oscars®	**Filming On A Microbudget**
Bruce Lee	**Film Music**

TV:

Doctor Who

Literature:

Cyberpunk	**Philip K Dick**
Agatha Christie	**Noir Fiction** (£2.99)
Terry Pratchett	**Sherlock Holmes**
Hitchhiker's Guide	**Alan Moore**

Ideas:

Conspiracy Theories	**Nietzsche**
Feminism	**Freud & Psychoanalysis**

History:

Alchemy & Alchemists	**The Crusades**
American Civil War	**American Indian Wars**
The Black Death	**Jack The Ripper**
The Rise Of New Labour	**Ancient Greece**

Available at all good bookstores or send a cheque (payable to 'Oldcastle Books') to: **Pocket Essentials (Dept CE), 18 Coleswood Rd, Harpenden, Herts, AL5 1EQ, UK.** £3.99 each unless otherwise stated. For each book add 50p postage & packing in the UK and £1 elsewhere.